1006745077

S0-EAJ-301

STORIES from the HEART

A Reading and Writing Book for Adults

Ronna Magy

Linda Mrowicki, Editor

LINMORE PUBLISHING   Box 1545   Palatine, IL 60078   (800) 336-3656

Linmore Publishing, Inc.
P.O. Box 1545
Palatine, IL 60078
(815) 223-7499

© Linmore Publishing, Inc. 1991
First printing, 1991
Printed in the United States of America

All rights reserved. No part of this book may be reproduced or transmitted in any form or by any means, electronic or mechanical, including photocopying, recording, or by any information storage or retrieval system without the written permission from the publisher.

STORIES FROM THE HEART
Student's Book ISBN 0-916591-26-3

Photo credit: page 14, International Institute of Rhode Island

Dedication

This book is dedicated to my parents, **Esther and Irvin Magy,** whose thoughtful admonition, "keep on going," has guided me through the new and challenging task of writing this book, and to my grandmother, **Minnie Hutton,** from whom I learned to care and to listen.

Acknowledgements

I wish to thank those who have served as my teachers: **Jackie Black, Frances Eisenberg, Linda Francois, Beverly Galyean, Dr. Douglas Holmes,** and **Bertie Segal.**

Marcia Chan, Francine Filipek Collignon, Connie Josef, Linda Kahn, Billie Lee Langley, Barbara Martinez, and **Barbara Sanchez** made thoughtful contributions to the work as it developed and gave me ongoing support.

Peggy Dean made sensitive additions and suggestions to the work. I also wish to thank **Sally Granick** for her skilled assistance in production.

My special thanks go to all the students at **South Gate Adult School** for the generous sharing of their life stories and to the faculty and staff there for their unfailing support.

This book would never have come to fruition without the openess, persistence, clarity, and caring of **Linda Mrowicki,** the publisher.

INTRODUCTION

Stories from the Heart is a reading and writing book for adults. The text consists of six units: About Me, Early Memories, An Important Experience, An Important Person, Problems and Choices, and Plans for the Future. The authentic student stories in the book are lively, compelling, and interesting. Student readers are easily drawn into the stories and are comfortable working with them. The stories are written by ESL students in adult education programs. Editing of the stories has been limited to correction of grammar mistakes which would affect the ability of the reader to comprehend the writer's message. Thus, the stories reflect the writers' experiences while modeling good reading and writing practice.

Each lesson consists of a story, followed by a reading comprehension check, a language focus, and a cooperative learning activity that focuses students on a specific issue raised in the story. The "About You" pages reformulate the issues raised in the stories so that individual student readers may draw on their own life experience in writing sentences and then, a paragraph about themselves.

Each unit concludes with a writing activity which uses imaging. Guided Imagery is the creating of pictures and/or sensations of experiences in the mind. The pictures or experiences may have occurred in the past, in the present, or might be something the students would like to experience in the future. The teacher may select one of the two Guided Images to read to the students. These images are the basis of the following individual composition practice.

Stories From The Heart incorporates current learning theory and practice in its approach. The text adheres to a whole language philosophy in that the content of the book is continually related to the students' own experiences and beliefs. Furthermore, as an ESL text, all four language skill areas - listening, speaking, reading, and writing are carefully integrated. Cooperative learning activities are built into the lessons to allow the sharing of information and experiences, peer teaching/learning, practice in a variety of group processes, and the opportunity to acquire oral language in a meaningful context. A "whole brain" approach is used in the writing of students' own stories at the end of the unit. The imaging activities allow the right brain (the creative side) to focus on an experience which the student can then express in writing through a variety of right and left brain (analytical) activities. The text also encourages the use of a process writing approach in which each student's story evolves through a series of stages of drafting, peer feedback, another drafting, peer editing, peer/teacher correction, and final writing.

HOW TO USE THE BOOK

The following are suggestions from the author on how to use the book. Teachers should feel free to adapt the material in the book to their own teaching styles and to each individual class of students.

The stories provide reading practice and introduce an issue which students can react to and discuss. Recommended steps for using the stories are:
1. The teacher focuses students' attention on the title and the photo. The teacher asks students what they think the story will be about.
2. The teacher presents any vocabulary words which are likely to be new to the students and which will affect the students' ability to comprehend the story.
3. Students read the story silently.
4. The teacher asks general comprehension questions about the story and reviews any difficult vocabulary words.
5. Oral reading is optional depending upon the students' desire for additional oral practice or the teacher's decision to do miscue analysis. One successful activity is to divide students into pairs and have them read the story out loud to a partner.

Check Your Understanding is a written exercise which focuses the student first on the main idea or author's intent and then on the comprehension of important details. Suggested steps are on the following page.
1. Students individually answer the questions.
2. The teacher checks the accuracy of the answers by either reviewing individual responses, checking the answers as a class, or using a cooperative checking.

Language Focus provides practice in grammar, punctuation, and vocabulary, thereby improving students' mechanical accuracy. This section is designed to enhance other "language" activities being pursued in the classroom. In this exercise, students fill in the blanks, sequence words in sentences, and search out word meanings. Group checking or whole class checking may be organized by the teacher.

Cooperative Activity is a small group discussion or pair work. It is designed to focus students on a poignant issue raised by the story. It may be a group discussion, a "Take A Turn", a Brainstorm, a ranking activity, or a story retell. In many of the activities, students are grouped in three's or four's and participation of each group member is essential. Following some of the activities, the small group's information is shared with the whole class orally and/or on the chalkboard.

Specific steps for the various **cooperative activities** are:

Discussion - Students sit in a small circle of three or four. A recorder/participant is designated for each group. Each student gives his or her opinion in response to each question. The teacher calls on several recorders to share the group's responses with the class.

Brainstorm - Students sit in a small circle of three or four. The recorder lists the ideas of the group. The entire activity has a time limit of five to ten minutes. Recorders then stand up and share their lists with the class or write them on the chalkboard and read them to the class. The teacher points out any similarities or differences or invites students to point them out or prioritize them in some way.

Take A Turn - Students sit in a small group. Each student has two minutes to respond to the question found in the book. The teacher acts as a timekeeper.

Story Retell - Students in a small group are designated A,B,C, or D. Each is given a part of the story to retell. They explain what they have already read to the group. While they may need to review the story before they do the retell, the oral work here is to retell the story in their own words.

Ranking - Working individually, students number a list of items in their order of importance. Then, they compare their lists with a partner or in a group and discuss their reasons.

About You, the last section of each lesson, encourages the students to tell and then write their own personal experience. The steps are:
1. Students talk with a partner about a topic introduced by the story, for example, a trip they took, a holiday they celebrated, or leaving their home country.
2. The students answer questions about themselves on the same topic.
3. The students write a paragraph using the responses to the questions.
4. The teacher should read the paragraphs and make suggestions for improvement.

END OF UNIT WRITING

GUIDED IMAGERY is a way of tapping into the mind of the student. It is a way of freeing/loosening the mind and allowing students to remember their pasts and dream the future. Imaging may be initiated by the teacher in a caring, sensitive way at the end of each unit.

1. **Selecting or writing an image:** The teacher should sensitively select one of the two images at the end of the unit based on his or her knowledge of the students in the particular class. Alternatively, the teacher may also ask the students for input on which of the two images they would prefer to do. For example, in Unit Four, "An Important Person", some refugee students may feel more comfortable talking about their present teacher, than they would remembering an adult from the past. The teacher should select the image which best suits the class. It is essential that the teacher read the image before doing it in the classroom. If there are any new vocabulary words, the teacher may change them to vocabulary known to the class or teach the new vocabulary so that it is comprehensible input at the time of the imaging. Imaging is listening and picturing practice - it is *not* a time to teach new vocabulary.

2. **Introducing the imaging activity:** Read this section out loud to your class, slowly. It is designed to introduce the students to the images.

3. **Breathing, centering, focusing, relaxing**: Begin each guided image with this slow, deep breathing and relaxing practice. Tell your students:
Close your eyes ... Breathe in ... Breathe out... Breathe in fresh air ... Breathe out any tension you may be holding in your body ... Breathe in slowly ... Breathe out slowly ... Sit comfortably in your chair ... Continue breathing ... Feel your feet on the floor ... Feel your hands on your desk ... Feel the top of your head ... your face ... your neck ... Let yourself relax ... slowly ... Relax your shoulders ... arms ... hands ... your chest ... stomach ... legs ... ankles ... your feet... Let out all the tension in your body ... Say to yourself, "I am now relaxed."

4. **Reading the Image:** Read the image slowly and with pauses. Each series of dots (...) represents at least a five second pause in voice time, allowing the students' minds to focus on the images as they develop. (Remember that the students are listening to you in a second language. Allow them the time to process what they are hearing and to create pictures from it.)

5. **Processing:** After the images are completed, allow students ample time to slowly open their eyes. Some may want to share in the class what they experienced. Next, let each student tell a partner about what they saw, heard, felt, tasted and experienced. Ask questions such as, "Where were you?", "What did you see?", "How did you feel?", "What happened?". The students will tell very detailed stories with vivid descriptions. Each student is allowed the right "to pass" if he or she does not wish to share the experience orally.

FIRST DRAFT: The students now write the first draft of their compositions. The teacher should provide a lot of encouragement for students to expand their ideas on paper. For example, if someone writes that they lived in a small house, the teacher could ask them to describe what it looked like inside and outside. This is a writing, stretching, and expanding stage.

PEER FEEDBACK and FIRST REWRITE: In this stage partners read their compositions and give feedback on what they would like to know more about and have clarified. Then, incorporating their partners' ideas, students rewrite their stories.

SECOND PEER FEEDBACK: Working with a partner, students are given suggestions on corrections of punctuation, spelling, capitalization, and grammar. The composition is corrected and handed in to the teacher.

TEACHER FEEDBACK: The teacher then corrects the paper for grammar, punctuation, spelling, and capitalization and returns it to the student.

FINAL VERSION: The student writes the composition on the final page of the unit and reads it to the class or a small group of other students. The other students ask questions about the composition. On the copy of the final version, the teacher can write personal notes to the student such as, "I understand how you feel " or, "What an exciting experience! I wish I could have been there ", thereby responding to the content as well as to the form.

NOTES FROM THE AUTHOR

Stories from the Heart brings living stories of adult immigrants and refugees to the classroom. The stories represent students' life experiences both past and present along with their hopes and dreams for the future. As a teacher, I have often found myself searching for ways to help my students tell their own life stories. I think that is the work of a true teacher - to facilitate students telling their own experiences, from the heart, in spoken and written English. By experimenting and using the language in its fullness to tell about themselves, students can truly become a part of their new country. It is my hope that **Stories from the Heart** will open up the hearts and minds of other students so that they, too, may tell their stories in written English. Then, these stories also can be shared with others.

I have often found that the acquisition of reading and writing skills depends more on the loving, caring attitude of the teacher and teacher encouragement than on any specific classroom techniques used. This book gives suggestions based on what has worked in my classroom, but often, a few words of encouragement, such as, "That's a good idea, keep on writing," or a question, "What happened then?" helps a student to focus and progress better than any specific technique. A short conversation at a student's desk as I read his or her incomplete composition will often help the student to finish a story on paper that is temporarily stuck in his or her mind.

For me, the reward of teaching reading and writing in a personal way has always been the delightful stories that flow from students' pens, the stories of life in other lands where I've never traveled, or of dreams I've never dreamed. Because of their writing, I am able to see life through their eyes.

Ronna Magy

CONTENTS

ABOUT ME

STUDENTS' STORIES:

ABOUT MY FAMILY

by Georgette S. Shenouda

Georgette with some of her family

My name is Georgette. My husband's name is Sabri. We are from Egypt. We have five children, four boys and one girl. The oldest child is Sherif, the second is Mary, the third and fourth are twins, Eid and Rouchdi, and the youngest is Mervy. Sherif is eighteen years old. Mary is seventeen years old. The twins are sixteen years old and Mervy is fifteen. The oldest has a job in a restaurant and goes to school to learn Spanish. The other children are going to high school and they have jobs in restaurants, also.

My husband works in a factory making electric lamps. I have no job because my English is not very good. My children are working part-time jobs. I go to school to learn English. I will get a job later.

We live in my husband's friend's house now. Someday we want to go to Texas nearer to my brother-in-law. He is a doctor. We want to buy a house there. We want our children to go to college and my husband wants to get a new job. I want to go to high school and then, train for a job.

CHECK YOUR UNDERSTANDING
Draw Georgette's family tree.

Georgette

| wife | husband |

| son | daughter | son | son | son |

Answer the questions with complete sentences.

1. Who is the oldest child? _____

2. How old are the twins? _____

3. What does Georgette's husband do? _____

4. What does Sherif do? _____

5. What does Georgette want her family to do? _____

_____

6. What does Georgette want to do? _____

LANGUAGE FOCUS
Fill in the correct words. Use "has" or "is".

Georgette _____ from Egypt. She _____ five children. Sherif _____

eighteen years old. He _____ a job in a restaurant. Her youngest child _____

fifteen. Georgette's husband's name _____ Sabri. He _____ a job in a factory.

COOPERATIVE ACTIVITY
Discuss these questions in a small group. Then, share your group's answers with the class.
1. Why do you think Georgette's oldest son is studying Spanish?
2. Why does Georgette think it is important for her family to move to Texas?
3. How does Georgette want her family life to be?

ABOUT YOU

Talk with a partner about your family. Tell your partner their names, ages, and other important information.

Draw your family tree.

Answer the questions with complete sentences.

1. Who is in your family? _____

_____

2. How old is each family member? _____

_____

3. What does each of them do? _____

_____

Write a paragraph about your family.

_____

_____

_____

_____

_____

_____

ABOUT MY EDUCATION

by **Marco Antonio Alvarez**

I was born in Mexico twenty years ago when my dad, Pablo, and my mom, Luisa, decided to have one more child. I am the youngest of their three children and the most beautiful of them, too.

I went to school in my country for thirteen years. I actually finished junior high school in Mexico. Then, I went to high school. I finished one year of high school. That was my last year at school in Mexico. I stopped going to school because I came to the U.S. When I got here, I went to high school for about six months. I was in the tenth grade. Then, I dropped out because it was necessary for me and my family to get more money from somewhere. That's why I stopped going to school and got a job instead.

CHECK YOUR UNDERSTANDING
Which school did Marco finish? Put a check in the correct column.

	Finished	Did not finish
Elementary school	✓	
Junior High School		
High School in Mexico		
High School in the U.S.		
Adult School		

Answer the questions with complete sentences.

1. How many years did Marco go to school in Mexico? _____

_____

2. When did he drop out of school in Mexico? _____

_____

3. Why did he drop out of school in Mexico? _____

_____

4. Why did he drop out of school in the U.S.? _____

_____

LANGUAGE FOCUS
Put periods in the correct places.

Marco was born in Mexico He's the youngest child in his family He went to school in Mexico for thirteen years He only attended high school in the United States for six months He went to work to make money for his family Now he has returned to adult school

COOPERATIVE ACTIVITY
Read the questions and brainstorm a list of reasons in a small group. Then, share your group's lists with the class.
1. Why do students drop out of school?
2. Why do people go to adult school?

ABOUT YOU

Talk with a partner about your education. Tell your partner the names of the schools you went to, the locations, and other important information.

Which schools have you attended? Put a check in the correct column.

	Attended	Did not attend
Elementary School	_____	_____
Junior High School	_____	_____
High School	_____	_____
Technical School	_____	_____
Adult School	_____	_____
College	_____	_____

Answer the questions with complete sentences.

1. How many years have you gone to school? _____

2. Why did you stop going to school? _____

_____

3. Why did you start adult school? _____

_____

Write a paragraph about your education.

_____

_____

_____

_____

_____

_____

ABOUT MY JOB

by **Roberto Valle**

I have been working in the same company since 1980. My first day of work was on May 4, 1980. I'm a machine operator. I work with other people on the same machine. I work the third shift. I work from 11:00 P.M. to 7:30 A.M. My days off are Saturday and Sunday. I take my first break at 1:30 A.M. or 2:00 A.M. Then, I eat my lunch. After that, I take my last break. In conclusion, I take two breaks plus my lunch. I'm going to try to get on a different shift in two weeks.

I like to work for this company because I have good benefits. I haven't had to pay the doctor bills for me or my family for a long time because I have medical insurance that pays the bills. I make good money, but I would like to work during the day.

CHECK YOUR UNDERSTANDING
Write the information from Roberto's story.

Roberto's Job: _____

Hours: _____

Benefits: _____

Pay: _____

Number of days off: _____

Number of breaks: _____

Answer the questions with complete sentences.

1. Why is Roberto happy with his job? _____

2. What does Roberto like about his present job? _____

_____

3. What would Roberto like to change about his present job? _____

_____

LANGUAGE FOCUS
Fill in the blanks with the correct preposition. Use "on," "from," "to," or "at."

Roberto began working _____ May 4, 1980. He works the night shift _____

11:00 P.M. _____ 7:00 A.M. His first break is _____ 1:30 A.M. He eats lunch

_____ 1:30 A.M. _____ 2:00 A.M. The night shift is over _____ 7:30 A.M.

The day shift on Roberto's job is _____ 7:00 A.M. _____ 3:00 P.M. Roberto's paid

vacation will start _____ July 15 and end _____ July 30.

COOPERATIVE ACTIVITY
Discuss the question in a small group. Then, share your group's answers with the class.

What makes a job "a good job" that someone wants to keep?

ABOUT YOU

Talk with a partner about your daily work. You may want to talk about your work at home or at school. Describe what you do, what you like about your work, and other important information.

Answer the questions with complete sentences about your daily work.

1. What work do you do everyday? _____

2. How many years have you done this work? _____

3. Are you paid? _____

4. If you are paid, are you satisfied with the pay? _____

5. What do you like about your work? _____

_____

6. What would you like to change about your work? _____

_____

Write a paragraph about your present work.

_____

_____

_____

_____

_____

_____

_____

_____

_____

_____

ABOUT THE PLACES WHERE I LIVED

by **Marie Liccioni**

I was born in Saigon, South Vietnam. My father was French and my mother was Vietnamese. I was the oldest child in a family of fifteen. I had six brothers and nine sisters. I do not remember my country very well because I left at the age of eight for France. I lived in Paris for awhile. It is there that I went to school and where I learned about art, literature, painting, fashion and cooking. I love Paris for the culture and the history of the city. This city is gorgeous. Wherever you go, you will always find something interesting. Paris lives day and night.

After ten years in Paris, my father bought a house in the southeast of France in Biarritz. It is there that I began to love the ocean and the countryside. The countryside holds no secrets for me. I was familiar with nature, animals, and plants. I learned to milk cows, make butter, etc. I had a lot of friends who were farmers.

At the age of twenty-one, I decided to move to Brussels, Belgium. Since then I have worked on many different jobs. From my life experiences came my love for travel. I have traveled all around the world. In between my work and my traveling, I gave birth to a girl, Sandra. She still lives in Brussels today. I live in Los Angeles now.

CHECK YOUR UNDERSTANDING
Write the names of the cities and countries where Marie has lived.

1. _____

2. _____

3. _____

4. _____

5. _____

Answer the questions with complete sentences.

1. Why does Marie not remember Vietnam very well? _____

_____

2. What did she like about Paris? _____

_____

3. What did she like about Biarritz? _____

_____

LANGUAGE FOCUS
Write sentences by putting the words in the correct order.

1. was born - Marie - in South Vietnam

_____

2. and - She - six - sisters - brothers - nine - had

_____

3. today - and - Her daughter - in Belgium - lives there - was born - she - still

_____

COOPERATIVE ACTIVITY
Work in a small group. Each person takes a turn answering the question.
(Two minutes per person.)
If you could live anywhere, where would you like to live? Why?

ABOUT YOU

Talk with a partner about the places where you lived. Describe where you lived and when you lived there.

Write the names of the cities and the countries where you lived. Include the place where you live now.

_____

_____

Answer the questions with complete sentences.

1. When were you born? _____

2. What city were you born in? _____

3. Did you grow up in the same place where you were born or did you move? _____

_____

4. What other places did you live in? _____

5. How long did you live in each place? _____

6. Which place did you like the best? Why? _____

_____

Write a paragraph about the places where you lived.

_____

_____

_____

_____

_____

_____

_____

_____

_____

MY LIFE IN MY NATIVE COUNTRY

by **Soukthavy Chanthavisouk**

I'm from Laos. I would like to tell you about my country. The terrain in this country ranges from lowlands to highlands, from jungle-covered mountains and fertile land to beautiful desert islands along the Mekong River. The people have been involved for many years in power struggles between various factions for government control.

The free education that was available was provided at all levels, but it was limited. The opportunity to receive a higher education was not always possible because the government did not have adequate educational resources such as materials, facilities, and faculty. I attended school from when I was six years old in Grade 1 until I was in Grade 12. When I graduated from high school, my parents supported me to continue my education in college for three years. I did not finish my college degree because my parents arranged for me to marry.

CHECK YOUR UNDERSTANDING
Put an X next to the things Soukthavy remembers about her country.

_____ mountains   _____ education

_____ weather   _____ government

_____ jungles   _____ medical care

_____ cities   _____ housing

_____ rivers   _____ transportation

Answer the questions with complete sentences.

1. Where was Soukthavy born? _____

2. What does she say about problems in her country? _____

_____

_____

3. How long did she stay in school? _____

4. Why did she quit school? _____

_____

LANGUAGE FOCUS
**Find the words in the story. Work with another student and write a definition.
If you do not understand a word, ask another student or use a dictionary.**

1. terrain _____

2. jungle _____

3. fertile _____

4. faction _____

5. faculty _____

COOPERATIVE ACTIVITY
**Work in a small group. Each person takes a turn describing his or her country.
(Two minutes per person.)**
1. What is your native country?
2. What is your country like? (The land, mountains, rivers, weather, etc.)

ABOUT YOU

Talk with a partner about your native country. Describe the geography, government, and other information.

Answer the questions with complete sentences.

1. Where were you born? _____

2. Describe the geography of your native country or hometown. _____

_____

_____

3. Describe the government in your country. _____

_____

4. Describe the school system in your country. _____

_____

5. Was education free in your country? _____

6. How many years did you go to school in your country? _____

Write a paragraph about your native country.

_____

_____

_____

_____

_____

_____

_____

_____

HOMESICK

by **Esperanza Gonzales**

I was born in Managua, Nicaragua. It is a small city. I was born on July 18, 1950. When I was born, my father was a farmer and my mother was a seamstress. She also took care of her children.

I went to school for about sixteen years. I liked school because I had a lot of friends and I had such nice teachers. I completed elementary school, high school, and the university.

My first job was as a teacher in an elementary school and my pay was $850.00 a month. I came to the U.S. because I did not like the kind of government that my country had at that time.

I feel homesick when I think about my parents, about my friends, and about the big house I left. I feel happiest in the United States when I receive letters from my family and when my mother gives me a phone call.

CHECK YOUR UNDERSTANDING
Answer the question.

When Esperanza thinks about her life, what does she think about?

1. _____

2. _____

3. _____

4. _____

Complete the sentences.

1. Esperanza feels homesick when _____

_____

_____

2. Esperanza feels happy when _____

_____

_____

LANGUAGE FOCUS
Insert capital letters.

esperanza was born in managua, nicaragua. she was born in 1950. her father was a farmer and her mother was a seamstress. esperanza completed elementary school, high school and the university in her country. she came to the united states because she did not like the government of nicaragua. sometimes she feels homesick when she thinks about her family.

COOPERATIVE ACTIVITY
Read the question and brainstorm a list of reasons in a small group. Then, share your group's list with the class.
Why do people leave their home countries and come to the United States?

ABOUT YOU

Talk with a partner about your home country. Talk about when and why you feel happy, homesick, sad, or any other feeling. You may want to talk about holidays, weddings, birthdays, times of the year, foods, or other things you remember about your home country.

Answer the questions with complete sentences.

1. When do you feel happy? _____

_____

2. When do you feel sad? _____

_____

3. When do you feel homesick? _____

_____

4. When do you feel angry? _____

_____

Write a paragraph about your feelings and thoughts about your country.

_____

_____

_____

_____

_____

_____

_____

_____

_____

TO THE TEACHER

NOTE: Please take your students' life experiences and interests into account when selecting a guided image to use with the class. Remember also to pause at least five seconds when you see the " ... ".

GUIDED IMAGE 1: A ROOM IN YOUR HOME

Introduction to the imaging activity: In this part of the lesson, you will be thinking about a favorite room in your house.

* Close your eyes ... Breathe in ... Breathe out... Breathe in fresh air ... Breathe out any tension you may be holding in your body ... Breathe in slowly ... Breathe out slowly ... Sit comfortably in your chair ... Continue breathing ... Feel your feet on the floor ... Feel your hands comfortably on your desk ... Feel the top of your head ... your face ... your neck ... Let yourself relax ... slowly ... Relax your shoulders ... arms ... hands ... your chest ... stomach ... legs ... ankles ... your feet. Let out all the tension in your body ... Say to yourself, "I am now relaxed."

Let your mind go back to the place where you live now ... In front of you is your front door ... Open the door ... Go inside ... Go into the living room or a favorite room ... Look around you ... Notice the furniture in the room ... chairs ... couches ... tables ... lamps ... What colors are they? ... What materials are they made of? Find a favorite chair or couch and sit down ... Relax as you sit down ... Look at the walls ... Notice the windows ... Look at the things in the room that you like ... books ... pictures ... objects from your country ... Let yourself enjoy being in this room of your house ... Enjoy the comfort ... the colors ... the objects ... Now, slowly come back to the classroom ... Breathe in and breathe out slowly ... Open your eyes ... Now, share your image of a room in your house with a partner.

GUIDED IMAGE 2: A MEAL IN YOUR HOME

Introduction to the imaging activity: In this part of the lesson, you're going to eat a meal in your home. You'll be eating with the people you live with now or, if you prefer, with some other friends. Think of some food you like to eat and people you enjoy eating with.

* Read the "relaxing paragraph" from Guided Image 1 before beginning this image.

Now imagine you are at home ... You are going to eat a meal ... Around you are the people you live with now ... Sit down together with them ... Listen to them as they speak ... They are talking about the food ... Smell the food ... It's your favorite food ... Slowly taste the food ... It tastes wonderful on your tongue ... Chew it slowly and enjoy each bite ... Eat your meal slowly, enjoyably with the people in your home ... Look at each person slowly ... Notice who they are ... your husband or wife ... your children ... your mother ... father ... your sisters ... brothers ... your aunts, uncles or cousins ... your friends ... Notice how old they are ... What do they look like? ... What they are wearing? ... Listen to their words ... Enjoy your meal with them ... Look around the table again ... Notice the people ... Listen to their conversation ... Smell and taste the delicious food ... Remember your home and your meal ... Now, slowly come back to the classroom ... Breathe in and breathe out slowly ... Open your eyes ... Now, describe the meal to your partner.

TO THE STUDENT

1. Close your eyes. Listen to your teacher. Think about the image.

2. Share your thoughts about the topic with a writing partner.

3. Write your story on a piece of paper.

4. Share your story with your writing partner. Ask your partner what he or she liked and what he or she would like to know more about.

5. Rewrite your story on a piece of paper. Include your partner's comments.

6. Ask your writing partner to check your punctuation, spelling, capitalization, and grammar. Then, make your corrections.

7. Share your composition with your teacher.

8. Write your composition on the next page. Then, share it with the class.

EARLY MEMORIES

STUDENTS' STORIES:

MY FAVORITE DRESS

by **Delia Soriano**

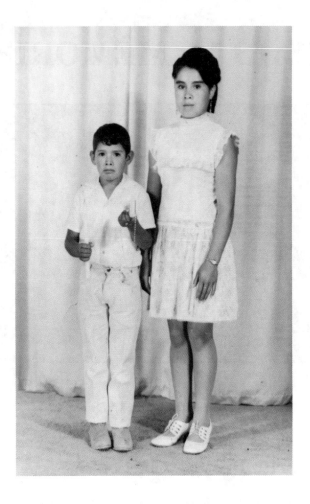

Delia when she was a child.

I remember when I was six years old. I always wore a dress when I went to school. My mother sewed beautiful dresses for me. My dresses were of different colors but I remember one of them. The color was orange. It had ruffles and a big bow on the back. Well, my dress was very beautiful.

CHECK YOUR UNDERSTANDING
Answer the question.

What did Delia want you to know about her dress? _____

_____

Circle the words that Delia uses to describe her dress in the story.

ugly	long	cheap
beautiful	expensive	store-bought
pink	cotton	second-hand
orange	wool	ruffles
black	hand-made	bow

Answer the questions with complete sentences.

1. How old was Delia in the story? _____

2. Who sewed her dresses? _____

3. How do you think she felt when she wore the dress? _____

_____

_____

LANGUAGE FOCUS
Insert capital letters and punctuation.

delia s mother sewed beautiful dresses for her delia remembers her favorite dress it

was orange it had ruffles there was a big bow on the back of the dress delia s mother

made this dress for Delia who was six years old

COOPERATIVE ACTIVITY
Discuss these questions in a small group. Then, share your group's answers with the class.
1. Why do you think Delia's mother made dresses for her daughter?
2. Why did Delia wear dresses to school and not pants?

ABOUT YOU

Talk with a partner about the clothes you wore when you were a child. Describe the type of clothing, the colors, and other important information.

What were your favorite clothes? _____

_____

Circle the words that describe your favorite clothes when you were a child.

white	blue	green	brown	yellow
orange	red	black	gray	violet
long	short	cotton	wool	rayon
hand-made	store-bought	new	second-hand	old
tight	loose	small	large	ragged
torn	faded	expensive	inexpensive	reasonably priced

Answer the questions with complete sentences.

1. Describe some favorite clothes you wore when you were a child. _____

_____

2. Did someone make the clothes for you or did someone buy them for you? _____

_____

3. Was your clothing the same kind that the other children wore or was it different? _____

_____

Write a paragraph about the clothing you wore as a child.

_____

_____

_____

_____

_____

_____

_____

_____

I REMEMBER MY FRIENDS

by **José G. Avila**

José and his baseball team

I was born in Zacatecas, Mexico. When I was a child, I liked to play in the river with my friends. Sometimes we were playing in the river for three or four hours. On our way home, we stopped to ride my neighbor's horses and he didn't like it. I remember one day when he told my father, "Your son took my horses when he came from the river. I hope that he doesn't do that anymore."

Then, my father spoke to me. He told me, "If you continue to ride the horses, we will have problems with the neighbor." My friends and I decided not to do it anymore.

Then, we formed a baseball team. The manager was our teacher. We practiced everyday for two hours. When we finished the game, we bought sodas. We drank them in the park. When I returned home, my father said to me, "Congratulations. You found a good sport." We played baseball for a long time. Later on, I left my city. We moved to Guadalajara, but I missed my friends on the baseball team a lot.

CHECK YOUR UNDERSTANDING
Complete the sentences by writing the correct letters next to each number.

1. At first, José and his friends _____

2. The neighbor _____

3. Then, José's father _____

4. Later, the boys _____

5. Their teacher _____

a. told him not to ride the horses.

b. formed a baseball team.

c. rode the neighbor's horses at the river.

d. was the manager of the baseball team.

e. talked to José's father.

Write the sentences in a paragraph.

_____

_____

_____

_____

_____

_____

LANGUAGE FOCUS
Fill in the blanks with "but" or "because".

1. The boys played in the river _____ it was fun.

2. The boys enjoyed riding the horses, _____ the neighbor did not like it.

3. The boys formed a baseball team _____ José's father advised him not to ride the horses.

4. José's father was proud _____ his son had found a new sport.

5. José liked Guadalajara, _____ he missed his friends in Zacatecas a lot.

COOPERATIVE ACTIVITY
Read the questions and brainstorm a list of games in a small group. Then, share your group's list with the class.
1. What games do children play indoors?
2. What games do children play outdoors?

ABOUT YOU
Talk with a partner about your childhood sports or games. Describe the games you played, your friends, and other important information.

Answer the questions with complete sentences.

1. Who did you play with when you were a child? _____

_____

2. Where did you play? _____

_____

3. What did you play? _____

_____

4. What did you like about playing the game? What didn't you like? _____

_____

5. Did your parents approve? Why or why not? _____

_____

Write a paragraph about a childhood sport or game.

_____

_____

_____

_____

_____

_____

_____

_____

_____

MY FIRST JOB

by **Alberto Villagomez**

In 1975 my family was very poor. We did not have any money to buy food. My father was sick. He couldn't work. Sometimes I saw that my mother was crying and I felt something bad in my heart. She did not see me when she was crying.

I went to talk with my brother. I explained to him what had happened with my mother. My brother told me that we needed to do something quickly. Then, we made two boxes to shine shoes. When we finished the boxes, my brother told me we had ten Mexican pesos. With that money we could buy things for cleaning and shining shoes. After we got the things, we left to go to the street to shine shoes. We made fifty Mexican pesos. Then, we came back to our house and we gave all the money to my mother. She was very happy.

CHECK YOUR UNDERSTANDING
Answer the question.

What did Alberto want you to know about his family? _____

_____

_____

Answer the questions with complete sentences.

1. What was the matter with Alberto's father? _____

2. What did Alberto see his mother doing? _____

3. What did Alberto and his brother do? _____

_____

4. How much money did they make? _____

5. What was their mother's response when she received the money? _____

_____

_____

LANGUAGE FOCUS
Fill in the blanks with verbs in the past tense.

Alberto's family _____ poor. They _____ enough money to

buy food. Alberto's father _____ sick. Sometimes Alberto's mother

_____ because there _____ no food. Alberto and his brother

_____ two shoe shine boxes. They _____ shoes and _____ fifty

pesos. Then, they _____ home and _____ the money to their mother.

She _____ happy.

COOPERATIVE ACTIVITY
Retell Alberto's story in a small group. Each person takes a part of the story. You can talk about who worked in Alberto's family, how much money they had, his father's health, his mother's sadness, the boys' solution to the family problem, and Mrs. Villagomez' reaction to the shoe shine money.

31

ABOUT YOU

Talk with a partner about a time when you wanted to buy something but you did not have enough money. (A car, a house, some furniture, a trip, etc.) Describe what you wanted, why you did not have enough money, what you did to get more money, and what happened.

Answer the questions with complete sentences.

1. What did you want? _____

2. How did you plan to get the money? _____

_____

3. Did you borrow money? _____

4. What happened? _____

_____

Write a paragraph about something you wanted to buy.

_____

_____

_____

_____

_____

_____

_____

_____

_____

_____

_____

1986

by **Michelle Penagos**

In 1986, I was fifteen years old. My mother was forty years old, my brother was six years old, and my sister was ten years old. I lived in San Salvador, El Salvador with my mother, my brother and my sister. We lived in a big house.

My mom worked in a government office. My brothers and I were in school. On weekends I played tennis and basketball at a club. That year I was very happy because my basketball team participated in a basketball championship and we won. It was very important for us because we worked together to win.

That year there was an earthquake in my country. It was at noon on October 12. A lot of people died and some buildings collapsed. My brothers and I were at school and when we got home, my mom was waiting for us. No one in my family died and my house was OK. It was not damaged, but that night we all slept in the garage because it was too dangerous to sleep inside the house. We were afraid of another earthquake.

That year I also celebrated my fifteenth birthday. It was a nice party. It was in a big church. My dress was long. The party lasted the whole night. I enjoyed it a lot. 1986 was one of the best years that I have ever had.

CHECK YOUR UNDERSTANDING

Write the three important things that Michelle wrote about.

1. _____

2. _____

3. _____

Answer the questions with complete sentences.

1. Where did Michelle live in 1986? _____

2. Why was it important when her team won the championship? _____

_____

3. When did the earthquake occur in El Salvador? _____

_____

4. What happened to Michelle's family during the earthquake? _____

_____

5. How did Michelle celebrate her fifteenth birthday? _____

_____

LANGUAGE FOCUS
Fill in the correct words. Use "was" or "were".

At noon on October 12, there _____ a large earthquake in El Salvador.

Michelle and her brothers _____ at school during the earthquake. They went

home. Her mother and brothers _____ alive. Everyone in her family

_____ safe. Their house _____ not damaged. They all slept in the

garage that night because they _____ afraid of another earthquake.

COOPERATIVE ACTIVITY
**Work in a small group and brainstorm as many natural emergencies as you can.
Who in your group has experienced them? When? What happened? Share your
group's discussion with the class.**

ABOUT YOU

Talk with a partner about a year which was important to you. Describe what happened during that year.

Answer the questions with complete sentences.

1. Which year are you thinking about? _____

2. How old were you then? _____

3. Where were you living? _____

4. Who were you living with? _____

_____

5. What were three important events?

_____

_____

_____

Write a paragraph about your life during that year.

_____

_____

_____

_____

_____

_____

_____

_____

_____

MY BROTHER AND ME

by **Alberto Villagomez**

When I was a child, I used to play with my older brother. We were very mischievous at that time. Sometimes people thought we were fighting, but we were only playing.

We used to play in an old and ugly room. There were lots of dangerous things in the room. One day while we were fighting, my brother pushed me back and I fell down on top of a glass bottle. I broke it with my arm. I didn't feel anything in my arm, but my arm was bleeding. We were very frightened because we were thinking about what happened. We did not know how to explain it to our parents. While we were talking in the room, my mom shouted to my brother. My brother left to talk to her and I said to him, "Don't tell her anything, please." My brother told me, "Don't worry, brother." When he came back to me, he told me, "Mom wants us to clean the yard." Then, we got an idea.

While we were cleaning the yard, I shouted, "Ay, Ay." Then, I ran to my mom. When my mom asked what happened, I said to her, "I fell down on top of a bottle." She was worried and we went to the doctor. The doctor sewed up my arm. My brother and I never fought again after that experience.

CHECK YOUR UNDERSTANDING
Draw a picture of Alberto playing with his brother.

Answer the questions with complete sentences.

1. Who was Alberto playing with? _____

2. Where were they playing? _____

3. How did Alberto cut his arm? _____

4. How did he explain his injury to his mother? _____

_____

5. What did Mrs. Villagomez do after she found out about her son's injury? _____

_____

LANGUAGE FOCUS
Fill in the blanks with "when" or "while".

_____ Alberto was a child, he played with his brother. _____ they

were playing, Alberto cut his arm. His arm was bleeding a lot. He did not know how to

explain what happened to his mother. Later, _____ he was cleaning the yard, he

shouted to his mother. _____ she saw his arm, she was worried. She took him to

the doctor.

COOPERATIVE ACTIVITY
Retell Alberto's story in a small group. Each person takes a part of the story. You can talk about Alberto and his brother, the room, Alberto's cut, their idea, and the visit to the doctor.

ABOUT YOU

Talk with a partner about something you did as a child that was not okay with your parents or another adult. (Fighting, breaking something, staying out late, etc.) Describe what you did, why you were not supposed to do it, and what happened.

Answer the questions with complete sentences.

1. What did you do? _____

2. Why weren't you supposed to do it? _____

_____

3. Who told you not to do it? _____

4. What happened to you after you did it? _____

_____

Write a paragraph about what you did.

_____

_____

_____

_____

_____

_____

_____

_____

_____

_____

_____

_____

MY HOMETOWN
by **Masako Onishi**

I was born in Hamamatsu, Japan. This city is located between Tokyo and Osaka. We have a wonderful network of railroads in Japan so we can get around on the famous bullet train. Hamamatsu is famous as a city of instruments. There are lots of instrument makers. They make pianos, organs, guitars and so on.

When I was a girl, my father was the manager of a company. Our family was living in wonderful conditions at that time, but my parents were already old and my brothers had already moved away to other cities. After I graduated from high school in Hamamatsu, I went to college in Tokyo. I have not lived in my hometown for thirty years. Of course, I go back to see my parents and brothers twice a year. I hope I will go to see my parents soon.

MY HOMETOWN
by **Xochitl Quezada**

My hometown is a very small town in Mexico. For me this was the best place to grow up. We knew everything about the neighbors. We were like a big family. The houses in this little town were big. They had many trees and flowers. When we woke up, the yards were permeated with the smells of different aromatic flowers. My preferred moments in my hometown were in the evening because at that time all the people were out on the sidewalks. The old people came out and talked. The children enjoyed playing out in the streets.

Later, we moved to Guadalajara, but we still went back to my hometown every weekend for a long time afterwards.

CHECK YOUR UNDERSTANDING
Compare Masako's and Xochitl's hometowns. Fill in the blanks with the correct information.

	Masako	Xochitl
Country:	_____	_____
Size of hometown:	_____	_____
People remembered:	_____	_____
Special memories:	_____	_____
	_____	_____

LANGUAGE FOCUS
Complete these sentences using the negative form of the verb.

1. Xochitl came from Mexico.

   Masako _did not come from Mexico._____

2. Masako lived in a city.

   Xochitl _____

3. Xochitl talked about the neighbors in her hometown.

   Masako _____

4. Xochitl wrote about the smells of the flowers in the yard.

   Masako _____

5. Masako goes back to see her parents twice a year.

   Xochitl _____

6. Masako went to school in Tokyo.

   Xochitl _____

COOPERATIVE ACTIVITY
Work in a small group. Each person takes a turn describing his or her hometown. (Two minutes per person.)
1. What do you remember about your hometown?
2. What changes have taken place since you left? (People, places, economy, etc.)
3. How do you feel about the changes?

ABOUT YOU

Talk with a partner about your hometown. Tell your partner about the name, location, and other important information.

Answer the questions with complete sentences.

1. Where did you grow up? _____

2. What do you remember about the hometown where you grew up? _____

_____

3. What do you remember about your neighbors? _____

_____

3. What sounds do you remember? _____

_____

4. What smells do you remember? _____

_____

5. What feelings do you remember? _____

_____

6. What tastes do you remember? _____

_____

Write a paragraph about your hometown.

_____

_____

_____

_____

_____

_____

_____

_____

TO THE TEACHER

NOTE: Please take your students' life experiences and interests into account when selecting a guided image to use with the class.

GUIDED IMAGE 1: YOUR HOMETOWN

Introduction to the imaging activity: In this part of the lesson, you're going to imagine returning to your hometown. If you lived in different places, pick the place you liked the best or you can think about the place where you live now.

* Close your eyes ... Breathe in ... Breathe out... Breathe in fresh air ... Breathe out any tension you may be holding in your body ... Breathe in slowly ... Breathe out slowly ... Sit in your chair ... Continue breathing ... Feel your feet on the floor ... Feel your hands comfortably on your desk ... Feel the top of your head ... your face ... your neck ... Let yourself relax ... slowly ... Relax your shoulders ... arms ... hands ... your chest ... stomach ... legs ... ankles ... your feet. Let out all the tension in your body ... Say to yourself, "I am now relaxed."

Imagine returning to your hometown or a place where you liked living ... In front of you is a familiar road ... an old road or a highway ... Do you see any people or animals or cars on the road? ... Notice any trees or plants along the side of the road ... Notice the weather ... Is it hot? ... cold ... raining ... Is the sun shining? ... What clothing are you wearing? ... Continue to walk down this road ... You are in your neighborhood ... Notice the houses ... What do they look like? ... Walk slowly until you come to your house ... Open the door ... Go in ... What do you see? What furniture is there? ... Sit down and listen to the sounds in the house ... Can you identify the sounds? ... Give yourself time to think about the good things that happened in the house ... times you laughed and felt happy ... times when you enjoyed yourself ...

Walk outside ... Walk down the street ... Notice any neighbors who are outside ... People you remember ... Notice what they are doing outside ... What smells are in the air? ... What sounds do you hear? ... Talk to a neighbor and find out the news of the neighborhood ... Begin slowly walking back to your house ... Notice the house ... the trees ... the flowers ... Walk down the road away from the house and your home town... Now, slowly come back to the classroom ... Breathe in and breathe out slowly ... Open your eyes ... Now, share with your partner your image of where you were, who you saw, and what you did.

GUIDED IMAGE 2: YOUR CHILDHOOD FRIEND

Introduction to the imaging activity: In this lesson, you're going to be thinking of an old friend, a friend you used to play with when you were a child. If you had several friends, pick the one you liked best. Think of a game you played together and where you used to play.

* Read the "relaxing paragraph" from Guided Image 1 before beginning this image.
Go back in time to your childhood ... a time when you were small ... a time when the world was large around you ... You are playing together with some friends ... Notice the game or sport you are playing ... You may be playing with a ball ... a doll ... a toy ... you may be playing a sport ... soccer ... baseball ... some other sport or game ... Take a moment to remember how you enjoyed playing with your friends ... Feel your happiness at being with them again ... Where are you playing? ... inside or outside ... How many people are you playing with? ... Look at one of your friends ... Is your friend the same size as you? ... taller ... shorter ... Is your friend the same age as you? ... What does your friend look like? ... What clothing is your friend wearing? ... Tell your friend how happy you feel to be playing together again ... Look at your friends ... Thank them for the fun you are having together ... Now, slowly come back to the classroom ... Breathe in and breathe out slowly ... Open your eyes ... Now, describe the game and your friends to your partner.

TO THE STUDENT

1. Close your eyes. Listen to your teacher. Think about the image.

2. Share your thoughts about the topic with a writing partner.

3. Write your story on a piece of paper.

4. Share your story with your writing partner. Ask your partner what he or she liked and what he or she would like to know more about.

5. Rewrite your story on a piece of paper. Include your partner's comments.

6. Ask your writing partner to check your punctuation, spelling, capitalization, and grammar. Then, make your corrections.

7. Share your composition with your teacher.

8. Write your composition on the next page. Then, share it with the class.

AN IMPORTANT EXPERIENCE

STUDENTS' STORIES:

MY FISHING TRIP

by **Gerardo Flores**

I lived in Sacramento eight years ago. One day, my friend invited me to go fishing. We went fishing on a river near Sacramento. My friend didn't tell me that I needed a fishing license. I didn't know it, either.

I saw a police officer coming over to us. The officer didn't speak Spanish. I didn't understand the officer. I hardly understood that he mentioned a license. I got out my driver's license. I showed him my driver's license. He thought that I was joking with him. He got very mad at me. He told me, "Listen to me, I need to see your fishing license." I felt scared to death. I thought he would put me in jail. He got out a book and wrote out a ticket. The ticket was very expensive because he thought I was laughing at him.

I went to pay the ticket. I never went to fish again after that. That was my first fishing trip. I haven't gone fishing again in my life. I have thought about going fishing, but then I'd have to buy a fishing license.

I wouldn't go fishing again without a fishing license because I had that experience. I'd recommend that you buy a fishing license before you try to go fishing.

CHECK YOUR UNDERSTANDING
Complete the sentences by writing the correct letter.

1. When the officer spoke in English, _____

2. When the officer asked for Gerardo's fishing license, _____

3. When the officer wrote out the ticket, _____

4. After Gerardo paid the ticket, _____

5. Before you go fishing, _____

a. he decided to never go fishing again.

b. you'd better buy a fishing license.

c. Gerardo felt scared to death.

d. Gerardo didn't understand him.

e. Gerardo showed him his driver's license.

Answer the questions with complete sentences.

1. Why did Gerardo decide to go fishing in the first place? _____

_____

2. Why did Gerardo show the officer his driver's license? _____

_____

3. Why did Gerardo feel afraid? _____

_____

4. What did Gerardo decide about going fishing in the future? _____

_____

LANGUAGE FOCUS
Insert the correct capital letters and punctuation.

gerardo lived in sacramento california he went fishing with a friend an officer asked

gerardo if he had a fishing license the officer did not speak spanish and gerardo did not

understand the officer's english the officer gave gerardo a ticket for fishing without a fishing

license gerardo has not gone fishing again after that experience

COOPERATIVE ACTIVITY
Work in a small group. Each person takes a turn speaking. (Two minutes per person.)

1. In what situations is it difficult for you to speak English?
2. What do you do in those situations? Do you ask someone for help?

ABOUT YOU

Talk with a partner about a situation in which it was difficult for you to communicate in English. (At work, school, the doctor's office, police station, immigration, etc.) Describe where you were, who you were talking to, what you were trying to communicate, and any other important information.

Answer the questions with complete sentences.

1. Where were you? _____

2. Who were you trying to communicate with? _____

3. What were you talking about? _____

4. What information didn't you understand? _____

_____

5. Were you able to get help in understanding the information? _____

_____

6. What happened? _____

_____

7. How did you feel afterwards? _____

Write a paragraph about your experience.

_____

_____

_____

_____

_____

_____

_____

_____

MY FANTASTIC TRIP

by **Adela Anguiano**

I remember all my family went to Yosemite three years ago. Yosemite is a big park. The trip was interesting. My husband drove about six hours. When we arrived, we found a big tree. In the park the trees smelled delicious. That was one of the things I liked.

We brought a ball, cards, and music. Near the tree was a lake where we went swimming, played, and danced. At night we lit a fire and made some coffee. My brother played a guitar. He played it and I sang. When everyone tried to sleep, a bear came up to us. We were so scared. My husband said, "Don't move and nothing will happen. The bear only wants food." Near the van was some meat. The bear took the meat and left. I also remember I bought a beautiful picture.

After three days we had to go back home because my husband and I had to go back to work the next day. We thought about taking another trip like this. We want to go to Acapulco for our next vacation.

CHECK YOUR UNDERSTANDING
Circle all the words you think describe Adela's trip.

boring   amusing   disgusting   confusing
exciting   fun   frightening   surprising
interesting   disappointing   shocking   exhausting

Answer the questions with complete sentences.

1. Where did Adela and her family go on vacation? _____

2. How did they get there? _____

3. What did they do after they arrived? _____

_____

4. What did the bear want? _____

5. Did Adela enjoy the trip with her family? _____

LANGUAGE FOCUS
Write sentences by putting the words in the correct order.

1. went - about three years ago - Adela - her family - to Yosemite National Park - and

_____

2. lit - a fire - at night - and - they - They - some coffee - made

_____

3. a guitar - Adela - played - Her brother - and - sang

_____

4. for three days - in the park - They - stayed

_____

5. next year - to Acapulco - They - to - want - go

_____

COOPERATIVE ACTIVITY
Retell Adela's story in a small group. Each person takes a part of the story. You can talk about their arrival and setting up camp, their evening activities, the bear, their leaving, and their plans for next year.

ABOUT YOU

Talk with a partner about a trip you took. Describe where you went, who you went with, and other important information.

Answer the questions with complete sentences.

1. Where did you go? _____

2. Who did you go with? _____

3. How long did it take to get there? _____

4. Were there any problems getting there? _____

5. Where did you stay? _____

6. What did you do? _____

_____

7. How did you feel about being there? _____

8. How did you feel about coming home? _____

Write a paragraph about your trip.

_____

_____

_____

_____

_____

_____

_____

_____

_____

_____

THE CHRISTMAS THAT ALMOST WASN'T

by **Mario A. Carrillo**

I had not seen my family for five years since I had come to the United States with the hope of getting a good education. Everything was going well for me, but I missed my family a lot. One December I decided to go to Mexico and spend Christmas with my family. I sent them a telegram letting them know that I would be arriving the 24th of December.

I started to buy all types of gifts for my sisters and brothers. I bought dresses, toys, and perfume. I spent all my savings. I was very excited about seeing them again. I missed hugging my mother and taking walks with my older brother.

Finally, the day arrived. The plane arrived on time. To my surprise, there was no one at the airport to welcome me. I took a taxi to my house. When I got there, all the lights were off. When I walked in the house, there was a tremendous feeling of emptiness. I could not understand what was happening. I wondered if they had received the telegram.

I went outside and sat down on the steps. Next to me were all the gifts I had bought for them. Around me, I could hear the sounds of families enjoying the holiday. I got up, and as I started to walk towards the street, I heard a soft voice calling my name. I slowly turned around, when all of a sudden, out of nowhere, all my brothers, sisters, nieces, nephews, and my mother jumped out from the darkness and shouted, "Surprise!"

What a wonderful surprise, and what a wonderful holiday, the Christmas that almost wasn't!

CHECK YOUR UNDERSTANDING
Answer the question.

What does Mario want to tell us about his holiday? _____

_____

Answer the questions with complete sentences.

1. Why did Mario come to the U.S.? _____

2. How did he feel about returning home after five years? _____

3. How did he prepare for his trip home? _____

_____

4. Who met him at the airport in Mexico? _____

5. How did he feel when he walked into the house? _____

6. What happened as Mario started to leave the house? _____

7. How do you think he felt about the surprise? _____

LANGUAGE FOCUS
Fill in the correct words. Use "no", "no one", "nowhere", "everyone" or "everything".

Mario had not seen his family for five years. He was excited about seeing

_____ again. When he went shopping, he bought _____ he could with

his savings. When he got to the airport in Mexico, _____ was there to welcome

him. When he got to his house, there were _____ lights on in the house. He

thought that _____ was home. Suddenly, out of _____, he heard his

name. _____ shouted, "Surprise!" It was a wonderful holiday for _____

in his family.

COOPERATIVE ACTIVITY
Discuss the question with a small group. Then, share your group's answers with the class.
Why is it important to be with friends or family on holidays?

ABOUT YOU

Talk with a partner about a holiday celebration in the United States or in your native country. Describe who you were with, how you celebrated, your feelings about being there, and other important information.

Answer the questions with complete sentences.

1. Which holiday did you celebrate? _____

2. Where did you celebrate the holiday? _____

3. Who did you celebrate the holiday with? _____

4. How did you feel about being with them? _____

5. Did you bring any gifts or food? _____

6. Describe the celebration. _____

   _____

7. How did you feel after the holiday celebration? _____

   _____

Write a paragraph about the holiday celebration.

   _____

   _____

   _____

   _____

   _____

   _____

   _____

   _____

   _____

MY ESCAPE FROM CAMBODIA

by **Loeun Bun**

I come from a small, suffering country known as Cambodia. I am nineteen years old. I have such a big family: four brothers and two sisters. I am the third one in the family.

Before 1975, I went to school in my country for four years. After that, there were no schools, businesses, religions, or hospitals because of political changes in the country. The new dictatorial leader, Pol Pot, a Communist leader, took charge of the entire country. People had to leave their homes, cities, towns, and villages to live on farms and in the forests.

After the evacuation of the cities, towns, and villages, they started to pick up the educated people and kill them without any reason at all. During those four years of hostility, I was separated from my family, friends, and relatives. This happened to every common person in the country. I decided to escape right away from my lovely country to find a new life in Thailand.

After seven years in a refugee camp in Thailand, I was accepted to come to the United States. First, I had to go to a refugee camp in the Philippines to study English for six months before coming here. After the completion of my class in the Philippines, I headed directly to the United States. Now, finally, I am here with my family in a foreign country and starting to face the obstacle of learning a foreign language.

CHECK YOUR UNDERSTANDING
Circle the correct answer. Then, write the answer on the line.

Loeun left Cambodia _____.
   a. to get an education
   b. to avoid being killed
   c. to learn a foreign language

Answer these questions with complete answers.

1. What political changes took place in Cambodia after 1975? _____

_____

_____

2. Where were people forced to move? _____

3. Who was killed by the government? _____

4. Where did Loeun escape to? _____

5. Where did he first study English? _____

6. What problem does he have to face in the U.S.? _____

_____

LANGUAGE FOCUS
Find the words in the story. What do the words mean? Work with another student and write a definition. If you do not understand a word, you can ask another student or use a dictionary.

1. killed _____

2. separate _____

3. escape _____

4. hostility _____

COOPERATIVE ACTIVITY
Discuss these questions in a small group. Then, share your group's answers with the class.
Can Leoun go back to his country now? Why or why not?

ABOUT YOU

Talk with your partner about your trip from your home country. Describe when you left, why you left, how long the trip was, and other important information.

Answer the questions with complete sentences.

1. Did you escape from or leave your country? _____

2. Why did you leave? _____

_____

4. Was it dangerous to leave? _____

5. How did you leave? _____

_____

6. How long did it take to get to the United States? _____

7. Are you with your family or separated from them? _____

Write a paragraph about why you left your country and your trip to the U. S.

_____

_____

_____

_____

_____

_____

_____

_____

_____

_____

_____

_____

STUDYING ENGLISH

by Oi-Chun Tung

When I was a child, I grew up in Hong Kong. I did not complete my education in Hong Kong. Everyday I walked about one and a half hours from home to school and back. Although it was a long walk, I enjoyed those days with my teachers and school-mates.

I remember the first time I studied English. The lesson was: "A man, a pan, a man and a pan, a pan and a man. This is a man." As I learned, I felt I was singing.

In my childhood I did not worry about anything. My parents took care of everything in my daily life. As I became older, I had more brothers and sisters. Life became harder for my parents. They did a good job raising us, but later, I needed to work. Before I came to the United States, I worked for about twenty years.

Now I am living in the United States. It does not seem as if I am in America. The reason is where I live. In the city where I live, a lot of people talk in Chinese. If I want to speak in English, I have to go to school. So, I spend my time in school. In my class, we all come from different countries. We have people from Mexico, El Salvador, Japan, Thailand, Korea, and Hong Kong. We are studying the same subject, "English as a Second Language". Even though our English is not enough to communicate well with each other, we use sign or body language to understand the meaning. When we have trouble communicating, the teacher corrects our pronunciation or meaning, etc. Now, I will stay here and continue with my studies. This is the best thing I can do for my future.

CHECK YOUR UNDERSTANDING
Answer the question.

What does Oi-Chun want to tell us about studying English? _____

_____

_____

Answer the questions with complete sentences.

1. Where did Oi-Chun first study English? _____

_____

2. Why does she say her first English lesson was like singing? _____

_____

_____

3. Why does she think it is important to study English as a Second Language now? _____

_____

_____

LANGUAGE FOCUS
Answer the question. Fill in the blanks with "she" or "her".

While Oi-Chun was living in Hong Kong, _____ studied English. _____

walked one and a half hours to school and back everyday. _____ English lessons were

like singing. _____ parents worked very hard while _____ was in school. After

Oi-Chun finished school, _____ worked for twenty years. Then, _____ came to the

U.S. _____ parents continued living in Hong Kong.

COOPERATIVE ACTIVITY
Read the questions and brainstorm a list of answers in a small group. Then, share your group's answers with the class.
1. Why do people study English?
2. Is English easy or difficult? Why?

ABOUT YOU

Talk with a partner about your experience with studying English. Describe the classes you took, your reasons for studying English, and other information.

Answer the questions with complete sentences.

1. Did you study English in your home country? Why or why not? _____

_____

2. Why are you studying English now? _____

_____

3. How long have you been studying English? _____

4. Where do you plan to use your English in the future? _____

_____

5. How will your studying English help you or your family? _____

_____

Write a paragraph about your experience studying English.

_____

_____

_____

_____

_____

_____

_____

_____

_____

TO THE TEACHER

NOTE: Please take your students' life experiences and interests into account when selecting a guided image to use with the class. Remember also to pause at least five seconds when you see the "...".

GUIDED IMAGE 1: VACATION

Introduction to the imaging activity: In this part of the lesson, you will be remembering a vacation or trip you have taken. It may have been in the U.S. or in your native country. Think about a place you enjoyed going to or a place you want to go to.

* Close your eyes ... Breathe in ... Breathe out... Breathe in fresh air ... Breathe out any tension you may be holding in your body ... Breathe in slowly ... Breathe out slowly ... Sit comfortably in your chair ... Continue breathing ... Feel your feet on the floor ... Feel your hands on your desk ... Feel the top of your head ... your face ... your neck ... Let yourself relax ... slowly ... Relax your shoulders ... arms ... hands ... your chest ... stomach ... legs ... ankles ... your feet. Let out all the tension in your body ... Say to yourself, "I am now relaxed."

Travel back to a place you have visited before ... a special place ... a place you have been to on a trip or vacation ... Look around ... Notice everything around you ... Where are you? ... What do you see? ... Are you in the city or in the country? ... Are there trees, mountains, or water near you? ... Are there cars? ... houses ... What sounds do you hear? ... Look around and notice everything important ... Notice the weather ... Is it summer or winter? ... Is it warm or cold? ... Notice your feelings about being on this trip ... Are you alone or with other people? ... What are you doing on this vacation? ... Are you visiting friends or family? ... Are you going to interesting places? ... Are you inside or outside? ... Take a moment and notice what you are doing ... Remember something special you enjoyed doing on this vacation ... a boat ride ... a walk ... a visit ... shopping ... Taste some special food you ate on the trip ... Remember how the food tastes ... Remember where you ate the food ... Now, slowly come back to the classroom ... Breathe in and breathe out slowly ... Open your eyes ... Share with a partner the image of your trip.

GUIDED IMAGE 2: A BIG CELEBRATION

Introduction to the imaging activity: In this part of the lesson, you will be thinking about a celebration. It may have happened in the past or it may be one that you would like to have in the future.

* Read the "relaxing paragraph" from Guided Image 1 before beginning this image.

Think of a time of celebration with your friends or family ... It is the time of a special celebration ... a holiday or an event ... a New Year's celebration ... a birth ... a wedding ... a ceremony ... a special time ... As you enter the room, notice any decorations on the walls or tables special for this occasion ... Pick up one of the decorations and hold it in your hands ... Do you hear any music playing? ... What kind of music? ... traditional music ... religious music ... special songs for the celebration ... Notice the special food for the celebration ... Look at its colors ... Smell it ... Put some food on your plate ... Taste it ... Notice the people in the room ... How much fun are you having together? ... Can you remember the fun of the occasion? ... How long is the celebration? ... Allow yourself to feel the happiness of this day ... the food ... the people around you ... the excitement of the celebration ... Now, slowly come back to the classroom ... Breathe in and breathe out slowly ... Open your eyes ... Share with a partner your image of the celebration.

TO THE STUDENT

1. Close your eyes. Listen to your teacher. Think about the image.

2. Share your thoughts about the topic with a writing partner.

3. Write your story on a piece of paper.

4. Share your story with your writing partner. Ask your partner what he or she liked and what he or she would like to know more about.

5. Rewrite your story on a piece of paper. Include your partner's comments.

6. Ask your writing partner to check your punctuation, spelling, capitalization, and grammar. Then, make your corrections.

7. Share your composition with your teacher.

8. Write your composition on the next page. Then, share it with the class.

AN IMPORTANT PERSON

STUDENTS' STORIES:

A SPECIAL FRIEND

by **Martin Garcia**

I have a special friend who I haven't seen for a long time. His name is Beimar. He is a native of the state of Chiapas in Mexico. Beimar and I were classmates at the University of Mexico.

Beimar was a pretty funny man. He was always smiling. He had a great sense of humor. He was a special person because of the way he looked. He was a short guy with long, curly hair. He usually wore jeans and boots. He walked in a very funny way because he was bowlegged.

He never organized his notes in school. He had only one notebook for all his classes, however, he was a very smart student because he only needed a few hours to prepare for a test.

I'd like to see him again. I don't know what has happened to him over the past few years.

CHECK YOUR UNDERSTANDING
Describe Beimar.

Height: _____

Hair: _____

Special physical characteristics: _____

_____

Clothing: _____

Personality: _____

Answer the questions with complete sentences.

1. Where did Martin meet Beimar? _____

_____

2. What kind of student was Beimar? _____

_____

3. Why do you think Martin was friends with Beimar? _____

_____

LANGUAGE FOCUS
Fill in the verbs.

Martin _____ a special friend who he hasn't seen for a long time. Martin and

Beimar _____ classmates at the University of Mexico. Beimar _____ a pretty

funny man. He _____ a great sense of humor. He _____ always smiling. He

_____ long and curly hair. He usually _____ jeans and boots. He _____

in a funny way because he _____ bowlegged. He _____ a very smart student

because he only _____ a few hours to prepare for a test.

COOPERATIVE ACTIVITY
In a small group, brainstorm a list of qualities you would like to have in "a good friend." Then, share your group's list with the class.

67

ABOUT YOU

Talk with a partner about a friend of yours. Describe your friend's appearance, personality, and other important information.

Answer the questions with complete sentences.

1. What is your friend's name? _____

2. Where did you meet your friend? _____

3. What does your friend look like? _____

_____

4. Describe your friend's personality. _____

_____

5. What do you and your friend like to do together? _____

_____

Write a paragraph about your friend.

_____

_____

_____

_____

_____

_____

_____

_____

_____

_____

_____

MY EX-GIRLFRIEND

by **Luis E. Martinez**

She was walking on the sidewalk that we used to walk on. She was wearing a beautiful pink dress. Her hair was loose. I called out to her and she turned around. She was happy and sad to see me. We walked until we reached a little park and started to talk. She asked me why we broke up. I told her the truth. I knew that she was dating another guy. We forgave each other because when I realized that she was dating another guy, I had dated someone else, too. I wanted to hug her, but my pride wouldn't let me do it. She was feeling the same way, too. Finally, we forgot what happened a few years ago and we began our relationship once again. I feel that I still love her.

CHECK YOUR UNDERSTANDING
Answer the question.

What is the topic of Luis' story? _____

Answer the questions with complete sentences.

1. Where did Luis see his ex-girlfriend? _____

_____

2. Describe her clothing and hair. _____

_____

3. Why did Luis originally break up with her? _____

4. Why did they forgive each other? _____

_____

LANGUAGE FOCUS
Write sentences by putting the words in the correct order.

1. Luis - on the sidewalk - his girlfriend - saw - walking

_____

2. her - He - and - around - turned - called - she

_____

3. to a park - walked - sat down - and - They - on a bench

_____

4. decided - their relationship - again - to begin - they - were sitting - in the park - While - they

_____

COOPERATIVE ACTIVITY
Discuss the questions in a small group. Then, share your group's answers with the class.
1. What makes people fall in love?
2. Why do they break up?

ABOUT YOU

Draw a picture of an encounter you've had with someone who you really liked. When you have finished drawing, label your picture. Then, discuss it with another student.

Answer the questions with complete sentences.

1. How did you meet each other? _____

_____

2. Describe what your friend looked like at the time you met. _____

_____

3. What interesting things did you do together? _____

_____

Write a paragraph about your first meeting.

_____

_____

_____

_____

_____

_____

_____

71

MY MOTHER

by **Eva Rodriguez**

Everybody is proud of their mother and I am not an exception. My mother is an excellent person. She is the best mother in the world. She is also my best friend. I always talk to her when I have a problem and she always gives me advice.

She is forty-three years old. She has short hair. Her eyes are brown. She is almost the same height as me. She is not fat, but now she is losing weight because she has a problem with her teeth and she cannot chew. She only eats soft food.

She works in a factory at night. She begins work at 3:00 P.M. and leaves at 2:00 A.M. It's hard work for her because she has to stand all the time and put blankets and towels into a big washing machine. She comes home very tired every day. Her days off are Wednesday, Saturday, and Sunday.

Her life has been difficult. She has always worked since we were children because my father died just eight years after they got married. She supported us while we were in school. She always wants the best for us. She is always worried about our food, our clothes, and our school. I know she wants us to have all the necessary things, therefore she works hard. I would like to help her and to help my brother. Therefore, I'm studying. I'd like to go to college and then, get a good job. If I did, she would be happy for the rest of her life. I really love her.

CHECK YOUR UNDERSTANDING
Fill in the blanks with information about Eva's mother.

Age _____   Job   _____

Eyes _____   Hours of work _____

Hair _____   Days off   _____

Medical or dental problems _____

Answer the questions with complete sentences.

1. What two jobs does Eva's mother have? _____

_____

2. How many hours a week does she work for pay? _____

3. Why does she work for pay? _____

4. Is Eva's mother married? _____

5. Who makes the decisions about taking care of her family? ____

_____

LANGUAGE FOCUS
Fill in the correct verbs.

Mrs. Rodriguez _____ forty-three years old. She _____ a single parent.

She _____ short hair and brown eyes. She _____ losing weight because she only

_____ soft food. She _____ the night shift in a factory. She _____ tired when

she _____ home from work.

COOPERATIVE ACTIVITY
Work in a small group. Each person takes a turn answering the questions. (Two minutes per per person.)
1. Why do men work? Why do women work?
2. Are there different reasons why people need to work?
3. What are some special problems single parents have?

73

ABOUT YOU

Talk with a partner about your mother, the woman who raised you, or another woman. Describe the responsibilities she had in the house, her jobs if she worked outside the home, and other important information.

Answer the questions with complete sentences.

1. Where did she work? _____

2. What was her job? _____

3. How many years did she work for pay? _____

4. What was her work at home? _____

_____

5. Who made the decisions about the family? _____

6. Was she happy about her job(s)? Why or why not? _____

_____

Write a paragraph about the woman's responsibilities inside and outside of the home.

_____

_____

_____

_____

_____

_____

_____

_____

_____

MY GRANDMOTHER AND MY OLDER BROTHER

by Patricia Cabal

Both my grandmother and my older brother were important people during my teen years. When I was ten years old, my mother died. My father had died before my mother. Then, my four brothers and I moved to Mexico City. We went to live in our grandparents' house.

My older brother was tall and thin and had blonde hair and green eyes like my father. He had to go from young to old quickly because suddenly, he had four children to support. I think it was very difficult for him because he wanted to enjoy his life as a young man but he had to be like a father to us. Maybe he wasn't as good as a real father, but he did it the best he could. He lost some girlfriends because he couldn't marry when the girls wanted to. He always said, "I am a single parent." One day he said, "Now it is my turn." Now, he is married and has three children.

The most important person was my grandmother. She was short and had dark hair, brown eyes, and a strong character. She brought me up. She taught me how to behave myself. Maybe when I was younger I thought she was wrong because she was such a hard woman and I had problems understanding her. Now, I know she did it well because without her I wouldn't be able to tell you what it was like to have a good grandmother.

CHECK YOUR UNDERSTANDING
Read the following statements about Patricia. Check if they "happened" or "did not happen".

	Happened	Did not happen
1. When she was a child, Patricia's parents died.	_____	_____
2. The children continued to live in their parents' house.	_____	_____
3. The children moved to Mexico City.	_____	_____
4. The children were brought up by their grandmother.	_____	_____
5. Her older brother went from young to old, suddenly.	_____	_____
6. Patricia's brother got married when he was a teenager.	_____	_____

Answer the questions with complete sentences.

1. Why did Patricia and her brothers move to Mexico City? _____

_____

2. Why did Patricia's brother become the "father" in the family? _____

_____

3. Describe her brother. _____

_____

4. Why did Patricia have problems understanding her grandmother? _____

_____

LANGUAGE FOCUS
Fill in the blanks with the correct preposition. Use "for", "in", "to," or "with".

While her parents were living, Patricia lived _____ Acapulco. Later, she moved

_____ Mexico City. She lived _____ her grandmother and brothers. Her

older brother became a father _____ the children. It was difficult _____ him to

be a father.

COOPERATIVE ACTIVITY
Discuss these questions in a small group. Then, share your group's answers with the class.
1. Do you know anyone who lost their parents when they were young children?
2. How can the loss of a parent affect the child?

ABOUT YOU

Talk with a partner about the person(s) who brought you up. Describe who they were, where you grew up, and other important information.

Answer the questions with complete sentences.

1. When you were a teenager, where did you live? _____

   _____

2. Who brought you up? _____

3. Describe the person(s) who brought you up. Give a physical description and also a description of their personality.

   _____

   _____

4. Did any adult you loved die when you were a child? If so, what happened?

   _____

   _____

Write a paragraph about the person who brought you up.

   _____

   _____

   _____

   _____

   _____

   _____

   _____

   _____

   _____

   _____

MY FATHER

by Isabel Royo

Although I was only six years old when I saw him the last time, I remember him very well. He was six feet, four inches tall and very handsome. The most important thing about him was his caring about people. My mother told me that he died in World War II when he was only thirty-three years old.

All my life I have tried to find relief for this loss of someone so important to me, but until now nothing has filled this great emptiness.

I detest wars because they aren't good for anybody. That war took away a dear, intelligent, and wonderful man: my father.

CHECK YOUR UNDERSTANDING
Answer the questions.

What does Isabel want to tell us about her father? _____

_____

_____

Answer the questions with complete sentences.

1. How old was Isabel when she saw her father for the last time? _____

_____

2. Which war did Isabel's father fight in? _____

_____

3. Who told Isabel that her father was dead? _____

_____

4. How does Isabel feel about her father's death? _____

_____

_____

LANGUAGE FOCUS
Find the words in the story. Work with another student and write a definition. If you do not understand a word, ask another student or use a dictionary.

1. loss _____

2. emptiness _____

3. caring _____

4. relief _____

COOPERATIVE ACTIVITY
Retell Isabel's story in a small group. Each person talks about one of Isabel's feelings. You can talk about Isabel's father, her love for her father, and her feelings about war. (Two minutes per person.)

ABOUT YOU

Talk with another student about your father, the man who raised you, or another adult man. Describe who he was, what he looked like, what you loved about him, and other important information.

Answer the questions with complete sentences.

1. What did the man look like? _____

_____

2. Describe his personality. _____

_____

3. What was his occupation? _____

_____

4. What was something you really enjoyed doing with him? _____

5. Is he still living? If so, where is he living? _____

_____

Write a paragraph about your father or another important man in your life.

_____

_____

_____

_____

_____

_____

_____

_____

_____

_____

TO THE TEACHER

NOTE: Please take your students' life experiences and interests into account when selecting a guided image to use with the class. Remember also to pause at least five seconds when you see the "...".

GUIDED IMAGE 1: SOMEONE I REMEMBER

Introduction to the imaging activity: In this part of the lesson, you will be thinking of a person who was important to you in growing up ... someone in your family or another adult.

* Read the "relaxing paragraph" from the Introduction, page iii, before beginning this image.

Bring to mind a picture or a feeling of a person important to you when you were growing up ... Someone who is still living now, or someone who has died ... someone for whom you have loving thoughts ... your mother ... father ... grandmother ... grandfather ... aunt ... uncle ... or any adult who helped you in growing up ... maybe someone who was not a part of your family...a friend ... Allow a picture of them to come into your mind ... Notice what they look like ... their face ... eyes ... hair ... the size of their body ... Notice their clothing ... pants ... skirt ... sweater ... blouse ... shirt ... dress ... maybe traditional clothing from your country ... How do you feel when you are with them? ... What smells or sounds do you associate with them? ... cooking ... animals ... machines ... perfumes ... musical sounds ... work sounds...

Share with them something about your life ... what you are doing ... what you are feeling ... Listen to them as they speak to you ... Listen to what they are saying ... Take a moment to talk with them ... Thank them for being with you ... for sharing with you ... Look at them again ... Notice how they are dressed ... what they look like ... smells in the air ... sounds you hear ... Notice how you feel with them ... Now, slowly come back to the classroom ... Breathe in and breathe out slowly ... Open your eyes ... Share with a partner who you saw, what they looked like, and what you talked about.

GUIDED IMAGE 2: MY TEACHER

Introduction to the imaging activity: In this exercise you are going to be thinking about a teacher ... It may be a teacher you have in school now, or a teacher you had in the past - someone who you enjoyed learning from.

* Read the "relaxing paragraph" from the Introduction, page iii, before beginning this image.

You are in a classroom ... a classroom where you have been before ... other students are in the room ... You are studying ... A teacher is in the room ... You feel excitement as you are studying ... Listen to the lesson ... What is the teacher talking about? ... English ... History ... Science ... Mathematics ... You listen to every word ... The lesson is important to you ... to your life and work ... You feel comfortable as you work in this classroom ... What does the teacher look like? ... What kind of person in your teacher? ... funny? ... serious? ... formal? ... relaxed? ... Talk with the teacher ... Ask a question about the lesson ... Listen as the teacher responds to your question ... How do you feel about learning? ... The teacher says that you are a wonderful student ... Take one moment and remember how much you enjoy learning there ... Tell the teacher your feelings ... how much you want to learn ... Now, slowly come back to the classroom ... Breathe in and breathe out slowly ... Open your eyes ... Share with a partner your image of your teacher, what he or she looked like, and what you talked about.

TO THE STUDENT

1. Close your eyes. Listen to your teacher. Think about the image.

2. Share your thoughts about the topic with a writing partner.

3. Write your story on a piece of paper.

4. Share your story with your writing partner. Ask your partner what he or she liked and what he or she would like to know more about.

5. Rewrite your story on a piece of paper. Include your partner's comments.

6. Ask your writing partner to check your punctuation, spelling, capitalization, and grammar. Then, make your corrections.

7. Share your composition with your teacher.

8. Write your composition on the next page. Then, share it with the class.

PROBLEMS AND CHOICES

STUDENTS' STORIES:

My Problem, Carmen Naval

My Problem, Maria E. Garcia

My Problem, Raquel Corona

My Problem, Roger Lopez

MY PROBLEM

by Carmen Naval

My son is sixteen years old. My husband loves his son very much, but he's a very strict father. Edward wants to go to the movies and go to parties with his friends. My husband says that it isn't safe for him to be out with his friends because when he goes out, his personality changes. For me, it's a wrong idea about Edward.

My son is a good boy. He studies in the tenth grade in high school. I think that he should have more freedom. My husband needs to talk with my son about life and explain what is dangerous for him and what is safe for him.

My son has his own personality, but my husband doesn't trust him. When I talk with my husband, I say, "Please try to talk and understand his age!" I want my son to be happy with us.

CHECK YOUR UNDERSTANDING
Write " T " if the information is true or " F " if the information is false.

1. _____ Edward is in the tenth grade in high school.
2. _____ Edward is twenty years old.
3. _____ Edward lives away from his parents.
4. _____ Mr. Naval, Edward's father, loves his son.
5. _____ Mr. Naval is an easy-going parent.
6. _____ Mr. Naval is very strict.
7. _____ The story is written by Edward's mother.
8. _____ Mr. Naval needs to talk to his son more and try to understand him.

Answer these questions with complete sentences.

1. How old is Edward? _____

2. What does Edward want to do in his free time? _____

_____

3. Why does Edward's father want to control his behavior? _____

_____

4. What does Edward's mother want her husband to do? _____

_____

LANGUAGE FOCUS
Put in the correct punctuation.

Edward asks his parents Can I go to a party with my friends

Edward's father says No, it is not safe

Later, Edward's mother talks to her husband She says Please try to understand Edward

COOPERATIVE ACTIVITY
Work in a small group. Each person takes a turn expressing her or his opinion about each question. (Two minutes per person.)
1. What should sixteen year olds be allowed to do?
2. What should sixteen year olds not be allowed to do?
3. Who should make decisions about what Edward can and cannot do?
4. Should Edward be allowed to do things in the U.S. that teenagers cannot do in his parents' home country?

ABOUT YOU

Talk with a partner about your experiences as a teenager. Describe who you lived with, who raised you, your activities, your friends, and other important information.

Answer the questions with complete sentences.

1. What problems did you have with your family when you were a teenager? _____

_____

2. Were your parents or the people who raised you strict or easy going? _____

_____

3. As a teenager, did you prefer to stay home or go out with friends? _____

_____

4. Were you ever punished or told you couldn't go out with friends? _____

_____

Write a paragraph about your experiences as a teenager.

_____

_____

_____

_____

_____

_____

_____

_____

_____

_____

MY PROBLEM

by **Maria E. Garcia**

I have a medical problem. I'd like to have a baby, but since 1984 I've been trying to have one and all the times I've tried were failures. I have seen many different doctors and the doctors have told me different things.

Last month the doctor told me that I have a little tumor in my uterus. The doctor talked to my husband about my problem and the doctor said, "It is because of this problem Maria can't have a baby, but don't worry." The doctor said, "I hope you can have a baby very soon."

Now, I have to go to the hospital to take many tests. The doctor told me that it is possible that I can have surgery to take out the tumor. Sometimes I feel sad and homesick because I need my mom in these moments. I hope someday to have a baby because it is my dream.

CHECK YOUR UNDERSTANDING
Answer the question.

What does Maria want to tell us about her problem? _____

_____

Answer the questions with complete sentences.

1. Who did Maria talk to about her problem? _____

_____

2. Why can't Maria have a baby? _____

_____

3. Why is Maria going to the hospital? _____

_____

_____

4. Why does Maria miss her mother? _____

_____

LANGUAGE FOCUS
Complete these sentences with "but" or "because".

1. Maria has been trying to have a baby, _____ she hasn't been successful.

2. The doctor told her she couldn't have a baby _____ she has a tumor.

3. She wants to have a baby, _____ she is afraid of surgery.

4. She feels sad and homesick _____ she wants to talk to her mother about her medical problem.

5. She wants to have a baby _____ it is her dream.

COOPERATIVE ACTIVITY
Discuss these questions in a small group. Then, share your group's answers with the class.
1. How does Maria feel about having a baby?
2. How important is it to have children?

ABOUT YOU

Talk with a partner about your last visit to a doctor. (If you haven't seen a doctor, talk about another member of your family or a friend who has).

Answer the questions with complete sentences.

1. What was the medical problem? _____

2. Did the doctor speak to you in English or in your language? _____

3. What questions did the doctor ask you? _____

_____

4. Did you understand the doctor? _____

5. Did you feel comfortable talking to the doctor? _____

6. Did you feel embarrassed? _____

7. Did the doctor give you any medicine? _____

8. How much did it cost to see the doctor? _____

9. Was the medical problem cured? _____

_____

Write a paragraph about the visit to a doctor.

_____

_____

_____

_____

_____

_____

_____

_____

MY PROBLEM

by **Raquel Corona**

I was thinking about my problem and I don't know if it's a real problem. Sometimes I spend too much money and then I feel guilty because I would like to save money. When I have extra money, I always think that I need to buy something new. I don't know why. Sometimes it's not necessary to buy something new. That's why I feel guilty.

I know that I need to save money because I would like to be prepared in case my sons want to go to college. My husband has a good income, but we have a lot of payments to make. When he gets extra money, we spend it.

I think the problem is because when I was a teenager I worked very hard and my mother took all my money. I never saw what she did with the money. So now, I always wish to have everything that I want immediately.

CHECK YOUR UNDERSTANDING
Circle the correct answer. Then, write the answer on the line.

Raquel's problem is that she _____

      a. has too much money

      b. spends too much money

      c. gives her money to her mother

Answer the questions with complete sentences.

1. How do you think Raquel felt when her mother took away all her money? _____

_____

2. Why do you think Raquel and her husband spend all their extra money immediately?

_____

_____

3. Why do you think Raquel feels guilty about spending her money now? _____

_____

_____

LANGUAGE FOCUS
Fill in the verbs.

When Raquel _____ a teenager she _____ very hard to earn money.

Her mother _____ all her money and never _____ any to Raquel.

Now, Raquel _____ her money as soon as she gets it. She _____ to save

money, but she can't do it. She _____ the problem comes from her teenage

experience with her mother.

COOPERATIVE ACTIVITY
Discuss these questions in a small group. Then, share your group's answers with the class.

1. Why do teenagers work in the U.S.? Where do they work?

2. Do teenagers work in your country? Why or why not? If they work, where do they work?

ABOUT YOU

Talk with a partner about a problem you had in the past that still continues. You can describe the problem, tell when it began, tell why it continues, and any other important information.

Answer these questions with complete sentences.

1. Describe your problem. _____

_____

2. Is it a problem between you and another person? _____

3. Where and when did the problem begin? _____

_____

4. What is a possible solution to your problem? _____

_____

Write a paragraph about the problem.

_____

_____

_____

_____

_____

_____

_____

_____

_____

_____

_____

MY PROBLEM

by **Roger Lopez**

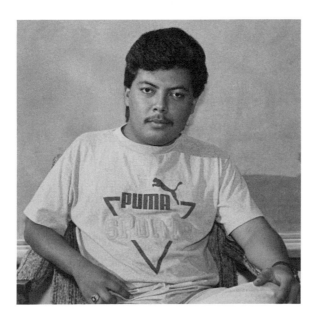

My problem is that I don't have any close friends who are my age. This is really hard for me because I don't have anybody who is my age to talk to like I usually did in Guatemala. Since I came here, all my friends are older than me.

I think that the problem began when I came here because I was just 18 years old. I couldn't be a student in a high school anymore. That was really what happened. I came here from a teenage school and when I got here to study I had to start in an adult school. Now, I usually have many friends but all of them are older than me. When my friends are at a party, they drink a lot of beer and I don't. I think we don't have anything in common.

My own solution to this problem is that I should go to places where other teenagers are. Then, I could meet some new people. I should go to a teenage group at church where I can find many boys who are my age.

CHECK YOUR UNDERSTANDING
Fill in the blanks with information about Roger.

	In Guatemala	In the U.S.
Friends' Ages	_____	_____
School	_____	_____
Where to Find Friends	_____	_____

Answer these questions with complete sentences.

1. How does Roger feel when he says, "I don't have anybody who is my age to talk to like I did in Guatemala?"

   _____

2. Who are Roger's friends in the United States? _____

   _____

3. How does Roger feel about his new friends in the United States when he says, "I don't think we have a lot in common"?

   _____

LANGUAGE FOCUS
Fill in the blanks with "he", "his" or "him".

Roger's problem is that _____ doesn't have any close friends _____ own age. _____ doesn't have anyone to talk with _____ about _____ problems. When _____ came to the United States, _____ was eighteen years old. All of _____ old friends were teenagers in Guatemala. Now, _____ is studying in an adult school. _____ needs to make some new friends.

COOPERATIVE ACTIVITY
Discuss these questions in a small group. Then, share your group's answers with the class.
1. Why is it hard to make new friends in a new country?
2. How can you make friends in a new country?

ABOUT YOU

Talk with a partner about your experience with making friends in the United States. Describe who your friends were in your country, how you met them, who your friends are now, how you met them, and other important information.

Answer the questions with complete sentences.

1. Who were your friends in your country? _____

_____

2. What did you like to do with your friends? _____

_____

3. Do you have close friends in the U.S.? _____

4. How did you meet them? _____

5. What do you like to do with your friends in the U.S.? _____

_____

Write a paragraph about your friends in your country and your friends in the United States.

_____

_____

_____

_____

_____

_____

_____

_____

_____

_____

TO THE TEACHER

NOTE: Please take your students' life experiences and interests into account when selecting a guided image to use with the class. Remember also to pause at least five seconds when you see the "...".

GUIDED IMAGE 1: A PROBLEM

Introduction to the imaging activity: In this part of the lesson, you will be thinking of a problem you have. It may be a small or a large problem. You will be thinking about a solution to the problem.

* Close your eyes ... Breathe in ... Breathe out... Breathe in fresh air ... Breathe out any tension you may be holding in your body ... Breathe in slowly ... Breathe out slowly ... Sit comfortably in your chair ... Continue breathing ... Feel your feet on the floor ... Feel your hands comfortably on your desk ... Feel the top of your head ... your face ... your neck ... Let yourself relax ... slowly ... Relax your shoulders ... arms ... hands ... your chest ... stomach ... legs ... ankles ... your feet. Let out all the tension in your body ... Say to yourself, "I am now relaxed."

Think about a problem in your life ... a new problem ... an old problem ... a family problem ... a medical problem ... a problem with friends ... money ... a problem with your job ... with immigration ... Focus like a camera on one problem that is bothering you ... Make a picture of the problem in your mind ... For one moment ... think about the problem ... Notice the way your body feels when you have this problem ... As you think about the problem ... bring to mind a friend or other person you can talk to about your problems ... someone from the United States or your home country ... someone living or dead ... Spend a moment and tell that person about your problem ... Now, listen as they talk to you about the problem ... Listen to their words ... to their voice ... Meditate on their advice for a moment ... Thank them for their advice ... Say good-bye to them ... Let them go on their way ... Now, slowly come back to the classroom ... Breathe in and breathe out slowly ... Open your eyes ... Share with your partner your image of your problem and your friend's suggestion.

GUIDED IMAGE 2: SOMEONE I KNOW WITH A PROBLEM

Introduction to the imaging activity: In this part of the lesson, you are going to think about someone you know with a problem. It may be a friend or someone in your family.

* Read the "relaxing paragraph" from Guided Image 1 before beginning this image.

Bring to mind a picture of someone important to you who has a problem ... someone in your family ... a close friend ... They are having a problem ... Listen as they explain their problem ... Is it a problem of relationships with others? ... a problem of health or money? ... a life problem ... What is the problem? ... Meditate for a moment on the problem ... (pause) ... How long has it affected their life? ... How has it affected their relationships with others? ... Has it stopped them from enjoying life? ... As a friend, make a suggestion to the person about how to understand the problem ... Suggest something that will help them think about the problem in a new way ... Spend a moment of time and talk with them about the problem ... Tell the person how much you care about them ... Now, slowly come back to the classroom ... Breathe in and breathe out slowly ... Open your eyes ... Share with your partner your friend's problem and your suggestions.

TO THE STUDENT

1. Close your eyes. Listen to your teacher. Think about the image.

2. Share your thoughts about the topic with a writing partner.

3. Write your story on a piece of paper.

4. Share your story with your writing partner. Ask your partner what he or she liked and what he or she would like to know more about.

5. Rewrite your story on a piece of paper. Include your partner's comments.

6. Ask your writing partner to check your punctuation, spelling, capitalization, and grammar. Then, make your corrections.

7. Share your composition with your teacher.

8. Write your composition on the next page. Then, share it with the class.

PLANS FOR THE FUTURE

STUDENTS' STORIES:

MY FUTURE

by **Raul Serrano**

I live in Maywood. I live with my father and my brother. My father is fifty-three years old and my brother is nineteen years old. My father spends a lot of time with us. He is a very good father. He worries about us.

I work for a company in Santa Fe Springs. I work from 3:00 P.M. to 12:00 A.M. I've been working for this company for six months. I like the work I do. They pay good money.

I have some problems that I need to take care of. I have lots of bills that I need to pay. Sometimes I would like to get another job, but I want to go to school, too. I don't know what to do. I'm confused.

My plans for the future are to get a better job, but first I need to speak the language and get my high school diploma. Once I've finished high school, I would like to become a fire fighter.

CHECK YOUR UNDERSTANDING
Answer the question.

When Raul looks at his life and responsibilities, how does he feel about:

1. His father? _____

2. His job? _____

3. Paying his bills? _____

4. Learning English? _____

Answer the questions with complete sentences.

1. How can Raul solve his money problems? _____

_____

2. What else do you think Raul needs to do for his father and his brother? _____

_____

3. What do you think he needs to do to get a high school diploma? _____

_____

LANGUAGE FOCUS
Find the words in the story. Work with another student and write a definition. If you do not understand a word, ask another student or use a dictionary.

1. confused _____

2. pay _____

3. diploma _____

COOPERATIVE ACTIVITY
Raul has six things he needs to do but he feels confused. Which do you think is the most important? Write the number "1" for the most important. Continue numbering the others in the order of importance. Then, compare your answers to those of another student.

_____ supporting his family   _____ going to school to study English
_____ looking for another job   _____ paying his bills
_____ getting a high school diploma   _____ finding personal satisfaction with his life

103

ABOUT YOU

Talk with your partner about your current responsibilities (family, home, work, school, etc.) Describe your responsibilities and your feelings.

Answer the questions with complete sentences.

1. When you think about your family responsibilities, how do you feel? _____

_____

2. When you think about your present job, how do you feel? _____

_____

3. When you think about paying your bills, how do you feel? _____

_____

4. When you think about speaking English fluently, how do you feel? _____

_____

5. When you think about your future plans, how do you feel? _____

_____

Choose an area of responsibility in your life (family, school, work, money, etc.) Write a paragraph about what you think and feel about this responsibility.

_____

_____

_____

_____

_____

_____

_____

_____

ABOUT MY CAREER

by **Maya Martinez**

I used to be a teacher in my country. I taught English in seventh grade in a junior high school. I usually worked alone, in fact, I like to work alone because it's faster and more convenient for discipline. I used to work only Wednesdays from 3:00 P.M. to 5:00 P.M. First, I began the class at 3:10. Then, I reviewed their homework. Next, I started to practice their reading and their writing. After that, we had a ten minute break and we continued the lesson until 5:00. On Thursdays I worked from 4:00 P.M. to 7:00 P.M. with two ten minute breaks and a thirty minute break for lunch. In Mexico the teachers do not receive good pay. I worked for $3.00 per hour.

I would like to be a teacher again. I'd like to work with teenagers, not small children. I like them because they are beginning to grow up and they are more responsible than little children. In that way I don't have to be a teacher and a baby-sitter. I'd like to teach in Mexico because the school where I was a teacher was very poor, but the kids wanted to learn. Sometimes they had to leave school because they had to work. That made me feel bad because they were too young to begin their adult lives. However, I still had a great time teaching.

In conclusion, teaching is a profession that gives you a lot of satisfaction, especially when the people who you teach are people who need you.

CHECK YOUR UNDERSTANDING
What was Maya's opinion of her teaching job? Put a check in the correct column.

	Liked	Disliked	No Opinion
1. Teaching small children	_____	_____	_____
2. Teaching teenagers	_____	_____	_____
3. Teaching as an occupation	_____	_____	_____
4. Students who left school to go to work	_____	_____	_____
5. Pay of $3.00 per hour	_____	_____	_____
6. Students who want to learn	_____	_____	_____
7. Her boss	_____	_____	_____

Answer the questions with complete sentences.

1. What type of school did she work in? _____

_____

2. What was her work schedule? _____

_____

3. What was her general feeling about her job? _____

_____

LANGUAGE FOCUS
Fill in the blanks using "at," "for," "in," "from," "on," or "to."

Maya used to be a teacher _____ her country. She used to teach _____ a

junior high school. She worked _____ Wednesdays _____ 3:00 P.M.

_____ 5:00 P.M. Her class began _____ 3:10 P.M. The students practiced

reading and writing with her _____ school. _____ Thursdays she worked

_____ 4:00 P.M. _____ 7:00 P.M. She worked _____ $3.00 per hour.

COOPERATIVE ACTIVITY
Discuss the question in a small group. Then, share your group's answers with the class.
1. How does Maya feel about being a teacher?
2. Why did Maya feel bad when her young students had to leave school and go to work?

ABOUT YOU

Talk with a partner about a job you would like to have in the future. Describe the job, work schedule, pay, your boss, and any other important information.

Answer the questions with complete sentences.

1. What job would you like to have? _____

2. What would the job responsibilities be? _____

_____

_____

3. What would your pay be? _____

4. What hours would you work? _____

_____

Write a paragraph about a job you would like to have in the future.

_____

_____

_____

_____

_____

_____

_____

_____

_____

_____

_____

MY FUTURE

by **Elizabeth Escoto**

I'm single. I live with my parents, my sister, and my brother who are studying in high school. My father's name is Roberto and my mother's name is Ana Maria. They are working. They are good parents. I love them very much and I am proud of my family.

My job is cleaning the house, cooking, doing the laundry, and picking up after my sister, my brother, and my mother. Sometimes I feel tired. I don't know why, but I haven't been sleeping very well.

Sometimes we have family problems, for example, last week my mother was very sick. She had a pain in her liver. She was in the hospital. At that time my family was very sad, but now she is better and she is working again.

My plans for the future are many. I want to buy a house for my parents. I would like to go to Mexico, to speak English very well, to get a good job, and I would like to travel, too.

CHECK YOUR UNDERSTANDING
Answer the question.

Which four topics does Elizabeth write about?

Paragraph 1: _____

Paragraph 2: _____

Paragraph 3: _____

Paragraph 4: _____

Answer the questions with complete sentences.

1. What chores does Elizabeth do around the house? _____

_____

_____

2. Why was Elizabeth very sad last week? _____

_____

3. What are some things Elizabeth would like to do in the future? _____

_____

LANGUAGE FOCUS
Fill in the blanks. Use "they are", "there are" or "there is".

Elizabeth lives with her parents, Roberto and Ana. _____ working.

_____ good parents. _____ two other children in the house, Elizabeth's

brother and sister. _____ a lot of work for Elizabeth to do at home. She cleans

the house, cooks, and does the laundry. _____ also some problems in the family.

Her mother has had medical problems. Now, she is better. _____ a

house Elizabeth would like to buy for her parents in the future.

COOPERATIVE ACTIVITY
Discuss this question in a small group. Then, share your group's answers with the class.
How can Elizabeth accomplish her future plans?

ABOUT YOU

Talk with another student about the home you would like to have in the future. You can describe the home, the location (city, state, or country), the rooms, and any other important information.

Answer the questions with complete sentences.

1. Where would you like to live (city, state, or country)? _____

_____

2. What kind of home would you like to have (an apartment, a condo, a house, etc.)? _____

_____

3. Describe the outside of the building. _____

_____

4. Describe the rooms. _____

_____

_____

5. Who would be living in your new home? _____

Write a paragraph about the home you would like to have in the future.

_____

_____

_____

_____

_____

_____

_____

_____

_____

SOMETHING ABOUT MY LIFE

by **Dominga Caballero**

My story begins many years ago when I was a student in my country. I was only twelve years old and I was the best student in my class because I always liked to study a lot. I got the highest score in my class and the school gave me a scholarship.

I was very happy and very excited because I wanted to be a doctor, but my father said, "No, you don't need to study more because you are a girl. Only boys need to study more." I felt frustrated and I cried a lot. Then, I had to work to help my family. I thought that when I had a daughter, she would be a doctor.

Several years after I got married, I came to this country. A few months later, I had my first child. She was a girl! Five years later, I had a boy. I worked very hard in a factory for twenty years. It was all to help raise our children.

During those twenty years I thought about my daughter and my wish. One year ago my daughter got her Bachelor of Science Degree in Biology from a university. It was at that time I decided to learn English because when she brought her friends to our home I felt embarrassed since I couldn't talk with them.

Now, I want to stay in school. I want to get my high school diploma. If God helps us, my daughter, who is now twenty two years old and a very intelligent girl, will go to medical school in September.

CHECK YOUR UNDERSTANDING
Complete the sentences by writing the correct letters.

1. When Dominga was twelve years old, _____

2. Dominga's father said, _____

3. After Dominga came to the U.S. _____

4. Dominga was embarrassed when _____

5. Her goal now is _____

6. Dominga's daughter will fulfill her mother's dream _____

a. to get her high school diploma.

b. she was the best student in her class.

c. by going to medical school in September.

d. she worked in a factory for twenty years.

e. "You don't need to study because you're a girl."

f. she couldn't communicate with her daughter's friends.

Answer the questions with complete sentences.

1. Why do you think her father told her that girls did not need to study? _____

_____

2. When Dominga thought about having a daughter, what was her wish for her daughter?

_____

3. When will her daughter begin to fulfill her mother's dream? _____

_____

LANGUAGE FOCUS
Fill in the correct words. Use "but" or "because".

1. She was very happy and excited _____ she wanted to be a doctor.

2. She wanted to go to medical school, _____ her father said she couldn't go.

3. Dominga felt frustrated _____ her father wouldn't let her continue in school.

4. She worked for twenty years in a factory, _____ she never forgot her dream.

5. She finally decided to go back to school to learn English _____ she couldn't communicate with her daughter's friends.

COOPERATIVE ACTIVITY
Retell Dominga's story in a small group. Each person tells a part of the story. You can talk about her scholarship, her wish to become a doctor, her father's decision, her job, her daughter, and her life today.

112

ABOUT YOU

Talk with a partner about your children or some other children who you are close to. Talk about what they look like, what they are interested in, what you love about them, and what your hopes and dreams are for them in the future.

Answer the questions with complete sentences.

1. What are the children's names? _____

_____

2. How old are they? _____

3. What do they enjoy doing? _____

_____

4. What do you want them to do when they grow up? _____

_____

_____

Write a paragraph about the children and your hopes for their future.

_____

_____

_____

_____

_____

_____

_____

_____

_____

_____

_____

MY PLANS

by **Erika Palencia**

I'm single. I live with my parents and two brothers. My father's name is Guadalupe and my mother's name is Delfa. My brothers' names are Guadalupe and Walter. We live in an apartment.

My parents and Guadalupe work. Walter studies in a junior high school. I'm working for a finance company. I'm just working part-time from 5:00 P.M. to 8:00 P.M. daily.

Sometimes I feel alone. I need to find a person who I can talk to. I'm planning to continue studying English to get my high school diploma. I want to take a computer course and then, study business administration. My plan is to work in a big company as a bilingual executive secretary.

CHECK YOUR UNDERSTANDING
Write the answers.

Write two facts about Erika now.

1. _____

2. _____

Write two plans has Erika has for her future.

1. _____

2. _____

Answer the questions with complete sentences.

1. What is Erika's present job? _____

2. What does she want to study in the future? _____

_____

3. What job does she want in the future? _____

_____

LANGUAGE FOCUS
Write sentences by putting the words in the correct order.
1. Erika - alone - Sometimes - feels

_____

2. a - Erika - needs - find - to - person - she - talk - who - to - can

_____

3. bilingual - plan - is - to - Erika's - work - a - in - company - as - secretary - big - a

_____

COOPERATIVE ACTIVITY
Discuss these questions in a small group. Then, share your group's answers with the class.
1. What are the advantages of being bilingual?
2. In what kinds of jobs is it important to be bilingual?

ABOUT YOU

Talk with a partner about what you want to do in the future. Describe what you are doing now and what you would like to do.

Write three facts about youself, your family, or your job, now.

1. _____

2. _____

3. _____

Write three plans that you have for your future.

1. _____

2. _____

3. _____

Write a paragraph about your present life and another paragraph about your future plans.

_____

_____

_____

_____

_____

_____

_____

_____

_____

_____

TO THE TEACHER

NOTE: Please take your students' life experiences and interests into account when selecting a guided image to use with the class. Remember also to pause at least five seconds when you see the " ... ".

GUIDED IMAGE 1: YOUR JOB

Introduction to the imaging activity: In this part of the lesson, you will be thinking about your job either inside or outside the home. If you are a student, you can think about your work in school.

* Close your eyes ... Breathe in ... Breathe out... Breathe in fresh air ... Breathe out any tension you may be holding in your body ... Breathe in slowly ... Breathe out slowly ... Sit comfortably in your chair ... Continue breathing ... Feel your feet on the floor ... Feel your hands on your desk ... Feel the top of your head ... your face ... your neck ... Let yourself relax ... slowly ... Relax your shoulders ... arms ... hands ... your chest ... stomach ... legs ... ankles ... your feet. Let out all the tension in your body ... Say to yourself, "I am now relaxed."

Think about your present job ... Watch yourself working ... Where are you? ... at home ... at school ... at a factory ... in an office ... at a hospital ... Notice where you are ... What are you doing? ... Are you making something? ... carrying something ... Are you inside or outside? ... Watch yourself as you work ... Are you alone or with other workers? ... Are you talking? .... thinking ... listening ... Is there anyone around you? ... Notice any sounds you hear ... noise of machines ... telephones ... cars ... What does it smell like where you work? ... Do you smell chemicals ... foods ... What smells remind you of your job? ... Do you stand, sit, or move around on your job? ... Is there a boss on your job? ... Is the boss talking to you? ... What does the boss say about your work? ... Take a moment, now ... Think of the things you like about your job ... What are some things you enjoy and appreciate? ... What are some things you don't like about your job? ... things that are problems for you ... Now, look around you at work, one more time ... Notice the work you're doing ... smells in the air ... sounds ... other people in the room ... Notice your feelings about your work ... Now, slowly come back to the classroom ... Breathe in and breathe out slowly ... Open your eyes ... Share with your partner your image about your job.

GUIDED IMAGE 2: FUTURE REFLECTION

Introduction to the imaging activity: In this part of the lesson, you will be thinking about making plans for the future.

* Read the "relaxing paragraph" from Guided Image 1 before beginning this image.

Picture yourself five years from now ... five years into the future ... Look at yourself ... Notice how you look ... Picture yourself on a job you want to be doing ... Where are you working? ... What are you doing? ... Now, go home ... Notice where you are living five years from now ... Look inside ... Allow yourself to feel satisfied with your home ... What are you thinking about? ... What is on your mind? ... What will be important to you? ... Who will you have special relationships with in five years ... family ... friends ... Take a moment and talk about your future plans with one of these special people ... Reflect again on ... your work ... your home ... your thoughts and ideas ... your friends and family ... your life five years from now ... Slowly, return to the present time ... Now, slowly come back to the classroom ... Breathe in and breathe out slowly ... Open your eyes ... Share with your partner your image of the future.

TO THE STUDENT

1. Close your eyes. Listen to your teacher. Think about the image.

2. Share your thoughts about the topic with a writing partner.

3. Write your story on a piece of paper.

4. Share your story with your writing partner. Ask your partner what he or she liked and what he or she would like to know more about.

5. Rewrite your story on a piece of paper. Include your partner's comments.

6. Ask your writing partner to check your punctuation, spelling, capitalization, and grammar. Then, make your corrections.

7. Share your composition with your teacher.

8. Write your composition on the next page. Then, share it with the class.